Trod the Stony Road:
A Young Man's Journey
from the Mississippi to
the Charles

Trod the Stony Road: A Young Man's Journey from the Mississippi to the Charles

Joseph F. West

2009

Trod the Stony Road: A Young Man's Journey from the Mississippi to the Charles

CHAPTERS

Brother-to-Brother: An Opening Dialogue

Don't Gather Fallen Fruit   3

Forged Steel   17

A Broken Beam   31

Pathfinder   39

Fear, the Terrible Thief   53

A Stuck Hog's Scream   61

And the Doors Slam to Open   71

On the Charles   81

Making the Turn Up   93

A Coda Blue   101

————————

Stony the road we trod,
Bitter the chast'ning rod,
Felt in the days when hope unborn had died;
Yet with a steady beat,
Have not our weary feet...

"Lift Every Voice and Sing"
—James Weldon Johnson

————————

But he who received the seed on stony places,
this is he who hears the word and immediately receives
it with joy; yet he has no root in himself, but endures
only for a while. For when tribulation or persecution
arises because of the word, immediately he stumbles.

—Mathew 13:20-21

BROTHER-TO-BROTHER:
AN OPENING DIALOGUE

Young man, you are, in my opinion, a bold light flickering with possibility—a possibility of making the impossible real, for shifting the world on its axis and quieting the absurd chatter of your demise. Though far too often than I care to recall we have come to be made painfully aware, that light has gotten dimmer. And there's some question as to not if, but how long until it is extinguished all together.

I'm not prone to street vernacular, and haughty or high-browed verbiage won't connect us. However, there is a challenge before you to navigate these words, digest them, and make them your own. I'm familiar with the ease with which you can do this. I've heard your rhymes. I've also witnessed your piercing glare as you've engaged obstacles and faced harsh winds. So I honor your strength.

Gird your loins, young man. You're neither pimp nor nigger, nor nigga' since the latter spelling somehow softens the blow. I know you find some comfort in these terms and some warmth in their vapid identities. They tend to shield you from the responsibility of claiming who you really are. But the hour has come to dismiss debasing caricatures and to shed reluctance.

Your journey of self-reclamation requires you to work. The purpose of the notes of this work is to strengthen and encourage you in your labors. To offer a tribute as you trod forward along life's undulating roads.

There are no smooth paths for men— only stony roads. Roads that must be traveled one step at a time.

DON'T GATHER FALLEN FRUIT

As a young male child of color, you feel
both blessed and burdened by your hue, and you
don't know what you'll pick up because of it.
What will stick to you and fill you up with the
goodness of purpose, or what will fester and
devour you with the sourness of indifference.

It's the low-hanging and fallen fruit, the
kind that drops to the ground and settles under
shadowy limbs, that's most tempting. Letting it
lie and rot for vermin and grubs to tussle over is a
lesson not easily learned.

As a child at the age of eight, I lived with
my father's sister, my aunt Jettie. Having no
children of her own, she adopted other children
in the neighborhood. Many Black children are
reared by extended family, for both audible and
silent reasons. I was no different. My father's
death from heart failure resounds as one cause,
and the unspoken concern of possible harm from
an unnerved mother was the other. So Aunt Jettie
was Momma West. She had plenty of help with
my cousins and me, as we all enjoyed the
company of my grandmother and my other aunts
and uncles.

Momma West welcomed me with a
mother's love, and though she had cared for me

frequently since my birth, this span was a most pivotal time. What I learned while having my hair soothingly brushed, or meticulously folding clothes, or attentively cooking, or enjoying a keen game of backgammon has steadied me. Her wisdom guided me through the tar pits and over the briar patches that would come. Prior to moving to Chicago, I lived with my father, mother, and three siblings in Eufaula, Oklahoma, where my family has deep roots. The kind of thick, interlocking roots that tie a people to land, hopes to labor, and dreams to familial bonds. Our roots were nurtured by the rebellious, independent spirits of love children born from Choctaw, Seminoles, and ex-slaves fleeing bondage in the Deep South. Stories of the 1921 Tulsa race riots, lynching, and land grab fueled a sense of self-determination in my kin that rode the rails all the way into Chicago.

Our last name West ties us to a paternal ancestor's insistence on renaming himself, claiming birth and right. Escaping chattel servitude and sharecropping, he scrubbed off a slave name with one speaking of a new direction, defying captivity of any sort. The strong will of Miles West, as imparted in family lore, serves as a pillar of my historical self-reference. Images of my ancestors carving out a life on the rugged, and racist, frontier inspire a deep sense of self-reliance in my family. In the West family, an unyielding faith fuels a stubborn commitment to service, and to each other. We learn the books of the Bible like we learn the alphabet. Faith has, for as long as

I can remember, also caused intense, if not all together calamitous, discord. And this, too, seeds and waters Love.

As a child in Eufaula, I lived just one block away from one of the country's largest manmade lakes, Lake Eufaula. The house we all lived in is still there—barely standing, but there nonetheless. I remember running barefoot down to the lake, jumping in the water, or racing along the docks where you could feed crappie and sand bass the size of small children. Now, in the summers, my two children get a kick out of the same thing. For a quarter you can purchase a handful of fish feed from a gumball machine, toss it into the lake, and marvel at the huge fish splashing and pushing to get to the surface.

In 1979, at the age of eight, I went back to Chicago to visit for the Thanksgiving holiday. This was when you could almost walk up to the counter at the airport, pay, and walk on just before takeoff. Like the children of parents during the Great Black Migration who sent their offspring off to Chicago, Detroit, or even St. Louis on trains with tickets pinned to them, I'd be placed in a seat and cared for by what were then called *stewardesses*. They were the ladies with wings. Funny now how as an adult I dislike flying, but as a child I found taking to the air magical. I would stare out the window from takeoff to landing, marveling at the patchwork of the country.

It felt good to land at Midway Airport and to hear the beat of the city and smell the rawness of the North. Momma West and my father's brother, Uncle Mike, were buzzing with excitement to see me when I landed. Leaving the airport we headed straight for some Chicago favorite eats, loading up on hot dogs, polish sausage sandwiches, fries with the skins on, and deep-dish pizza.

Momma West and Uncle Mike shared a house together. As we ripped open the bags, laid the spread out on the table, and began to reconnect and renew, some of their friends came by and a party started. It never took much to get one going. A little greasy, deep-fried Chicago victuals drizzled with the sauce of soul music was a nice way to return to what I always called home. Marvin Gaye, Curtis Mayfield, Stevie Wonder, Roy Ayers, Herbie Mann, or Earth, Wind and Fire and the cool wash of libations flowed with laughter and tales of community building and loves lost and gained.

At the tender age of eight, I could easily feel the energy of connectedness among divergent and like personalities bound by neighborhood history, Chicago politics, and an infectious joy for living.

We toured the city some, walked the neighborhood, and embraced the moment. Though I was connected to Oklahoma, Chicago held my heart. It was where the West family was, including my grandmother Phebe. There have been many stories of the Black matriarch who keeps the family centered, and with a simple smile, tender embrace, or terse scripture laden word commands the soul of the family. Phebe West was such a woman. That Black matriarch, woven so deep in the labyrinths Black family life folklore standing on the Word of God, dared anyone to try and move her from it. When I wasn't with Momma West I was with my grandmother listening and learning. And when I wasn't with my grandmother I was with one of my other aunts. I was surrounded by love and no matter what direction I turned it was there, pushing me forward, raising expectations, and lifting up prayers. My grandmother died my first semester of college. But for the prayers of my aunts and uncles, then and now, I doubt if I would be alive, let alone have realized any modest success in life.

Days passed with the heightened fervor of my return. Then, one day, things suddenly changed. The sun came up but had no warmth. Like a pierced balloon, the joy slowly seeped away. A few days after my arrival, we received news of my father's death. I knew I wasn't going back to Oklahoma.

I wanted to stay right where I was. I was afraid that without my father or being closest to those most intimately tied to him, I'd be swept under an approaching current, never to see the surface. I didn't quite know what it was, I just knew it was out there, lingering, rolling my way. He was gone and I no longer had rails on either side against which to brace myself.

The burial of my father was contentious, with heavy questions and dark, quiet, slow-moving clouds surrounding his death. I held my feelings inside and let the questions settle in the back of my heart, encased in imperfect resolve and later in budding self-discovery.

Over the years I would wrestle with what losing my father at such an early age meant. As a young man with bits and pieces of emotion, stories, and what I felt inside, I started to put together an image of him. I tried to recreate the man and step inside the image. It fit like an oversized suit, and I grew into it hoping I got the proportions correct all the while making alterations along the way. It was never a perfect fit. I just wanted him covering me enough to never fall off.

***

My sense of drive, commitment to social justice, and pursuit of excellence all comes from the lessons my Momma West taught me. A staple and driving force in the community, as an educator she has helped raise three generations of young people on Chicago's Westside. She has been a teacher, disciplinarian, parent, and friend to students at George W. Collins High School

since it first opened in the late seventies. At least
once a week, Momma West has a grateful former
student as a visitor. The school has since been
renamed, reorganized, and refitted with new
values. And like so many Chicago public schools,
it faces many challenges. As a kid, I would roam
the halls or play in the gym. The strong sense of
caring and community in that place still resonates
today whenever I walk through the building.

Momma West is a spirited woman, full-
figured and full of life. She is also very particular,
artistic and "shoots from the hip." Living with
her wasn't always easy; could have been her
meticulous nature, forthrightness, and high
expectations, but I suppose for a kid, parental
rules never are very easy to swallow. Of course,
once it's ingested you know it's good for you.
Momma West's motto for work was, "Go after
all in hopes of getting one." And her command to
me was, "Never gather fallen fruit. Always reach
for the best, the good stuff at the top." Reading
was one rule I had to follow, and I took to it
easily. She would ask, "What's the best way to
hide something from a Black man?" I would say,
"Put it in a book." Nothing was to be hidden
from me.

We had plenty of books, thick ones and
thin ones, books written by Black people, books
written by non-Black people, by Americans and
non-Americans. Poetry, history and literature of
all sorts were available for me to devour. There
were *Ebony* and *Jet* and newspapers like the

Chicago Defender, The Tribune, and every Chicago community's weekly story in print in our library. In addition to the printed word, I also learned to read my social condition, to become socially literate. Old Black Panthers with colorful names still committed to the school breakfast program, Black Revolutionaries still committed to social justice, street poets, philosophers, teachers, and shapers of the common man's language in prose, music, and song were all frequent visitors. If that wasn't enough, I could walk down the street to the house I live in now and talk with my aunt Naomi, who'd tell of meeting Marcus Garvey and the advice she'd give him, or how she listened to Martin Luther King but *heard* Malcolm X. She was, and still is, a walking world encyclopedia, an authority on the African Diaspora, Egyptian history, slave narratives, and Native American people.

North Lawndale is a strong community, and I have strong memories of its vibrancy from my childhood. On our block we had a Tuskegee airman, a former Negro league ballplayer, and elders drenched in the richness of the Civil Rights struggle. They all set expectations. They set boundaries and without trying commanded respect, and taught you to read.

Momma West subscribed to *Architectural Digest (AD)* and *GQ.* I was pretty sure we were the only Black folks on that part of town that did so. Both *AD* and *GQ* represented two unique perspectives she possessed and was determined to pass on. *AD* reflected her deep artistic side. This side allowed for hours of thumbing through the magazine looking at pictures of big homes and admiring the furniture, landscapes, and artwork. Long before cable shows made it chic to do so, she would translate some of these ideas into our home.

The purpose of reading *AD* was to stir the imagination. We didn't talk so much about how big the house was or the costs of things; instead, we imagined the story behind each spread. We'd discuss the places they were located, and she would make a point for me to imagine visiting them one day. "Just because you don't have lot of money doesn't mean you can't live well," she always said—and continues to say today. "Take care of what you have and live well with it."

While *AD* was about having fun dressing up the house, *GQ* was about dressing me up. We didn't have a lot of money, but every chance Momma West got to put a suit on me or replicate an outfit she'd seen in *GQ,* she took it. I'd fuss and stomp around not wanting to wear clothes that my friends didn't wear. "Don't gather fallen fruit," she'd say. "Anybody can get the stuff lying around. Want more. Want better."

So we reached a compromise. I would have two sets of clothes: one set were my "school clothes" and the other were my "street clothes." I would get dressed in my school clothes with the idea that I wasn't going to school to play. That school was about business, and I had better be prepared each day to take care of it. Right after school I rushed home and changed into my "street clothes," making sure I either hung up or folded my "school clothes." For the most part, I stuck with the compromise. However, there were a few times when the lure of a buzzing baseball diamond would seal my fate.

I love baseball. For as long as I can remember, I loved the Negro leagues and sometimes would pretend that I was "Cool" Papa Bell flying around the bases. If I was on third, I would pretend to be Jackie Robinson stealing home. Early one spring my Momma West got me a white linen suit. It was a suit clearly meant to be in the "school clothes" category. She had saved for the suit, and once she had it, must have showed it to twenty different people before I wore it.

Once I put the suit on, I felt like I was wearing a big eggshell. I could barely move without thinking I would crack it open, and then I'd spill out naked to the world. I ate breakfast, went to school, and got through lunch and two recesses without getting one speck of dirt on the suit. And then I headed home. After school I was to go to the sitter's house and wait to get picked up. I was also to change clothes as soon as I got there. I was halfway obedient. The sitter, Mrs. Lay, lived next to a nice big sandlot that served to us as Comiskey Park, home to the White Sox.

As I was walking down 15th Street, there was a lot of commotion and dust kicking up everywhere. I could hear the crack of the bat and the crunch of crushed pop can bases. We played with wooden bats and real baseballs. I tried my best to walk past the field, turn the corner, go inside, change clothes, and then come out and play. I waved to the guys playing, who were yelling my name and anxious for me to get on the field. I put up the "one-minute" finger indicating that I needed a minute to change clothes. But they kept yelling my name and saying how much they needed me to beat the guys from Douglas Boulevard. I was a good ballplayer, swift, and could catch anything. Sometimes I played second and shortstop—at the same time. A sandlot legend—in my own mind.

I then made the fatal mistake most young boys make. I started to believe my own mythical greatness, and my ego switched from Bell and Robinson to Josh Gibson. I didn't forget I had the white linen suit on, I just thought it would add to the legend. I vividly imagined I would step up to the plate, dig in my back foot, take a pitch or two, and on the third pitch hit a home run and stroll around the bases in my white suit like the Ghost of Gibson. "You won't even get dirty," my ego whispered in my ear. "They'll be talking about this for a hundred years."

I bit, and bit hard.

I laid my books down and came to the plate. The field was buzzing. I took the first pitch, then the second. Before he could hurl the third, I pointed to an abandoned Oldsmobile near the alley where I would deposit the ball. The third pitch came and I swung. The bat didn't quite sound like a home run crack, it was more like a poor dribbling get moving down the base path single crack. I was embarrassed. They were expecting heroics and here I was sending a dribbler down third and getting a single. I was determined to give them heroics.

My ego again chimed in. "It's OK," it said. "What we'll do is blaze around the bases and score, leaving so much dust behind you it won't even get on the suit." I was so focused on the word *score*, I didn't stop to think of how idiotic this really was. The next batter stepped up and I dug in, again. I was determined to score. The hitter swung and hit a line drive between second and first. I had already started running, so the ball whizzed behind me. I glided over second and tore into third determined to thunder down and reach home. I could hear everybody yelling slide, slide—the throw was coming, so I did—I slid into home in a cloud of dust—in my white linen suit.

I scored, we'd won, but there wasn't any cheering going on. It was eerily quiet, like someone had died—or, as I'd soon learn, was about to. I was still on the ground as I turned and looked at the field. All the players were looking out past home base into the street—past me. I turned my head to see what they were looking at. It was Momma West, sitting in her car with the most bewildered look on her face. She had watched me glide over second, tear into third, and thunder down to reach home—in my white linen suit.

I jumped up and started dusting myself off. Mrs. Lay and nearly half the block came out and pleaded for mercy on my behalf. "Oh, don't kill him. Don't kill him" Mrs. Lay cried out running to the car. It didn't work. My Momma West made me walk home as she sped ahead and waited for me inside. Needless to say I got a nice spanking, and on top of that she made me wash the clothes using an old stainless steel washtub and washboard. It felt like I was washing for days.

Some years later I came to appreciate the lesson this brought. The clothes she bought were meant to instill both a sense of responsibility and pride. Preparing for school was important, and I didn't have to settle for what everyone else wore, or to put a finer point on it, settle on everyone else's expectations. Today, I live but five houses down from Momma West in the same house where I'd come to listen to stories and arguments between Sox and Cub fans living under the same roof.

But, there are no more picture windows open to imagination. Blinds are drawn and curtains closed so as not to reveal what you possess and whether or not you're home. People no longer walk through the neighborhood, they stumble and wander. The magic is gone; folks have become unhinged.

Boys with pants hanging low and underwear showing walk the streets not like they've just escaped from a chain gang but as if they're rushing to get back to one. We've gone from "street clothes" to "gutter clothes." The "school clothes" are the uniforms worn by children attending the charter school, or the military-style khakis and white T-shirts that jarringly connote prison garb. Empty young men bore through the streets in cars, playing rude, nasty, and disrespectful music so loud it cracks the paint in homes and shakes windows so that you feel they'll shatter any minute. They are begging for attention at any cost. There are no men, only boys with guns, petty drugs, and the time—and the willingness—to kill. As kids we knew the police in the neighborhood. Occasionally, they'd stop and watch a good sandlot game. But as an adult, I fear them. You see the police cozy up to the drug dealers under the guise of investigation. Truth is, peace takes work and requires time, while drug dealers pay money.

One of the biggest pains to me is to see so many young men without anyone setting expectations of success for them. There's no one helping them understand that there are times when you must be serious about your presentation and your speech. And when you're ready to play, change into something more appropriate. There's a void of people who love my young brothers enough to broaden their imagination and encourage dreams of fancy places and the stories that come with them. Children without parents or parenting live on the scraps of love and togetherness, and there's not enough to go around. The hungry fight for whatever they can get, and like locusts ravage everything.

Granddad has faded from memory, and Grandma has stopped trying. She's tired and has no more stories to tell. Her house is paid for, so everybody has moved in—crowding her out. Her guilt and faith in God opens the doors and the floodgates to a new kind of heartache and disappointment. I can see her fighting to defend some ideal, some memory of family and saneness that once existed. But it's changed. Faded pictures of Martin Luther King, John F. Kennedy, and a White Christ on the Cross are but dusty dimples in the wall. She is overburdened with her children's children, and sometimes, her children's children's children.

The street poets have no rhyme, and the Griots are long gone. The Civil Rights movement is a myth, and Black history is the twenty-eight days you endure before the last snows start to fall. There's a self-loathing and self-pity that no pretty pictures in a glossy magazine, or even a wide-eyed, hopeful politician, can seem to change. It's deeper than we have the courage to address. The blood's memory has been erased. It used to be on Easter Sunday you'd see more three-piece suits on young boys than at an undertakers' convention. Now we don't even dress our sons up when they must be in the undertaker's hands, and God knows that's been far too frequent.

I understand what Momma West and hundreds of other mothers like her were trying to do for me and for their sons. They were fighting to combat and dispel myths and stereotypes about what a Black man was and could be. Momma West was protecting me against the pathology promulgated by misinformation and distorted images that flash haplessly on the tube and in print. From the foul stench of lies sold wholesale in corner stores, courtrooms, newsrooms, town halls and pristine legislative pews. Against the rot under the tree.

Although she takes pride in me, I see the sadness she feels for the likes of those I played ball with who have yet to thunder down and reach home. The lowest common denominator seems to have won, and whatever is lying about is fair game and edible.

Every day, I drive past that sandlot where we used to play. Now it's littered with broken glass, abandoned cars, and trash, instead of little boys with bullying egos racing around touching crushed pop-can bases and aching to become legends.

FORGED STEEL

I once was told by an old gandy dancer that some men are cast while others are forged.

Gandy dancers were the men, mostly Southern Black men, who stretched the railroad tracks across America. Some chose the occupation, while others were forced to work in prison chain gangs or as bartered debt. A gandy was a level used to thump rails into position to then be hammered down.

Gandy dancers worked in great rhythm, beating steel, body, heart, and song, connecting to the land, rail, and each other. Because it took so much to do so little for so long, patience and inner strength were the fabric woven into the belly-busting song of a gandy dancer that moved the line forward.

A fight erupted between Momma West and my momma. I was recalled, retracted to leave North Lawndale for East St. Louis where my biological mother had settled on her way to Texas, where her brothers and sisters lived. I was to be separated from my roots, ripped from what tied me to myself, to my father. No more trips to Oklahoma, no more stories, no dressing up, and no reaching out. An indescribable pain melded to my bones, making moving unbearable. Nonetheless, I went. One bag full of clothes and memories packed onto a Greyhound bus bound for St. Louis. I was nine years old. A few years had passed and I felt isolated, caged, because I had not spoken to anyone in Chicago since the day I boarded the bus south. All lines were cut.

I wanted to be back in Chicago where things were normal, where there was a consistent harmony between when you rose in the morning and when you lay down at night. A harsh discord was pounding away at my ears, and a new unsettling beat dominated. I was having a hard time falling in line and keeping up. I was slipping fast into a strange, unfamiliar place. The current had arrived, swallowed me up, and the light at the surface got thinner.

Then I met Mr. Gandy.

He was the shade of gray ore, his face peppered white by a short, shaggy beard. He was old, but blue-ox strong, with hands firm enough to drive a rail spike with his fists if he so chose. When we met he told me to call him Mr. Gandy, and this old dancer moved and spoke with such an ancient syncopation that you could hear in his words and feel in his eyes the polyphonic clang of steel and flesh.

He chewed tobacco and spit. "I know steel and iron, son," he'd say in a bluesy 4/4 beat that rolled from his mouth as smooth as a steam-powered locomotive. "Each metal has a unique tensile strength, a point at which it will bend, break, or be reformed under pressure."

I visited with him from time to time to hear the stories of his days working the rails, gambling, running liquor, and hunting women, rabbit, and deer. Sometimes I couldn't tell the difference between the women and the wild game. The stories were funny mostly, some sad, but all allowed me to escape. He lived near a shallow creek a few miles from my house in East St. Louis in a three-room shack.

One day while I was running along that creek, dodging in and out of trees and splashing through the muddy water, he appeared. I ran through the creek when things got really bad for me—and when I met Mr. Gandy, things were bad.

I actually learned about the creek late one summer and nearly lost my sight there while playing with some of the older boys in the neighborhood. They'd go up there and disappear for hours, and one day I tagged along. There are all kinds of games you can play in the woods, and boys seem to have a way of coming up with the ones that can cause you the most harm; these were also the ones that seemed to be the most fun.

Along the creek grew tall, bamboo-like stalks that we could pull up with our bare hands. The stalks had mud and roots packed at one end,

21

and we would throw them at each other. Even though the spears wouldn't impale you, if thrown hard enough they would definitely sting and leave a deep bruise. This was before paintball, but the idea was the same. There would be flags and fortresses, the goal being to capture the other team's flag.

I wasn't strong enough to throw the spears with the kind of velocity needed to compete with the bigger boys, but I could run and was elusive. So, I was a flag catcher. My orders were to run under cover of fire, climb trees, swing across the creek to the enemy's side, dodge fire, and capture the flag. On this particular day, our team was winning. We had managed to get close enough to the other team's flag, where a quick swing across the creek and a weasel-like dash would yield victory.

I dodged spears as I grabbed for the vines that would swing me across. My team gathered a bunch of spears and laid down heavy fire, and I leapt on the vines, kicking down a spear aimed at my legs. But with the kick I broke the vine and landed short of the banks on the other side; I'd have to crawl to reach the top and then run to get the flag.

I crawled up the bank staying low, spears whizzing by. I reached a fallen tree and crawled along thinking I could use it for cover, jump up, and run and snatch the flag.

Then suddenly, the action that was once intense had ceased. It had gotten quiet on both sides of the creek. I figured everyone was out of ammunition and had gone to reload. I looked back and saw it to be true; both teams were gathering up spears. No one had called time out, so I figured I could use this break to get the flag and we would win.

Unfortunately, I miscounted how many from the other team I saw gathering spears. There was one boy left with one spear, and as I peeked up from behind the fallen tree to get a clear view of the flag, I got nailed in the face.

Blood spewed everywhere. I was semi-unconscious and fell back, rolling down the banks and into the creek. Muddy water and blood blinded me, and I could hardly breathe. The biggest and strongest boy, named Junior, picked me up and raced me home. I was taken to the hospital where I stayed for a couple days. I had several surgeries to repair damage to my eyes and fix the broken bones around my nose. I was forbidden to play with these boys again or go back to the creek.

After lying around the house for several weeks, and missing some school, I knew I had to go back; otherwise I'd be done for in the neighborhood. I'd be labeled a "punk" and soft and couldn't go to school, let alone show my face at a ball field or basketball court. I'd learned this a few years earlier while in Chicago.

One summer day in Chicago, I was playing in our yard with my little cousin but wanted to go to the sandlot and play with some older boys. I begged and begged to go. Momma West said no repeatedly because she thought they were too rough and I'd get hurt. That made me really want to go, not because I wanted to disobey but because I wanted to prove that I couldn't be hurt.

Eventually I sneaked out of the yard and made my way down to the sandlot. I hadn't been there fifteen minutes before a really big kid split my nose. I cupped my nose and blood ran down my arm. I was screaming and crying and could hear them laugh as I ran home. Once I got home, Momma West cleaned me up, stuffed my nose with tissue, and sent me back down to the sandlot. This time I pleaded not to go. Playing in the yard with my cousin was what I wanted to do. She said no, since I had made up in my mind that I was going to be disobedient, I had to go back down there. I had to let the other boys know I wasn't scared; otherwise they would beat me up each time they had a chance.

After crying and putting on a dramatic display about not being loved and that I was going to die if I went down there again, I slowly made my way back with a nose packed full of tissue. A few yards before reaching the sandlot, I wiped my face, and with a bloodstained T-shirt stepped back onto the sandlot. The guy that

busted my nose the first time came over by me,
and I drew up my fists. As he got closer, out of
what might have been shock he burst into
laughter and put me on his team. I stayed and
played until dusk. So I revisited that creek,
sometimes by myself, sometimes with others; but
we never threw spears at each other again.
Following my incident, each time we played
"capture" we threw rocks—the logic of boys.

Mr. Gandy was carrying fish and looked
dogged tired when we met. I offered to help him
carry his catch home. I have always had an affinity
for old Black men. I always saw something surreal
in their eyes and could connect with them. It was
often said by loved ones that I had an old soul,
and perhaps that was the case. Mr. Gandy and I
would sit and talk some early mornings when I
sneaked out the house and ran along the creek.
He'd sit on a porch that leaned heavily, gut fish in
old newspaper, chew tobacco, and reminisce. He
never mentioned children so I assumed he didn't
have any. He treated me like a favorite nephew,
though. I would just listen.

He liked talking about steel. To him it
was what most Black men had to be made of to
make it in America. "To be cast, though
malleable, is to be formed under a low melting
point and composed of scrap iron. Casting
requires a lot of hand holding," he once said in
the high tone of an old philosopher. "Cast metals
don't act right when you put them under extreme
changes in hot and cold. And when placed under

pressure, all of the bubbles and impurities deform the metal and reveal all the weakness.

"You don't get that when you forge steel, though, son," he said, knifing a fish down the middle and scraping scales. "See, forged metal is made under pressure. A solid red-hot bar or pallet pressed, pounded, and squeezed under a lot of damn pressure to form one solid piece." He spit off to the side of the porch and looked up, dropping the knife to pull the insides of the fish out with his fingers. "Forged men are nothing like cast Negroes—there's no strength or character in them."

Stretching out his arthritic fingers and rubbing the back of his hands, he paused to look at me. "And when metal meets metal, it shows, son, it shows."

I often wondered whether I was forged or cast, and it wasn't until the age of fifteen, when a guy pointed a gun in my face because he thought I belonged to a rival gang, that I found out. There were two gangs in East St. Louis, the Vice Lords and the Black Gangsta Disciples. Where I lived, the Vice Lords ruled. This is when I learned about affiliation through association.

I never joined a gang. I didn't have an interest, and there was no pressure on me to join. However, many of the boys around me were hardcore members. Others were loosely involved, meaning that they kept enough distance to fight, but not kill; to steal, but not get caught; and to deal drugs, but not do the prison time.

Football, basketball, and baseball were also big in East St. Louis. Late one afternoon I'd arrived home from work with my stepdad, the real reason I called East St. Louis home. There were some guys headed to the diamond. I got permission to go play some baseball. So I rushed inside and threw on some baseball clothes, not being conscious of the colors. I grabbed my glove and ran out of the house, racing to catch up to the other guys. We played two great games, mixing the teams up and switching positions, stopping only to refuel on Mr. Pure juices, chips, and hot pork skins. Once it was near dark, we all headed home. I had some money on me and was still hungry.

For three dollars you could get a large order of fried rice and a soda from the Chinese food place that had a red and white sign that simply read "Fried Rice." The restaurant was the size of a small room, and you passed your money through the bulletproof glass and waited to get your food through a sliding drawer. I did that, and then went to a park a half a block away to watch some basketball. There were plenty of tricked-out cars and onlookers. I found a good spot under a tree, ate, and watched budding basketball stars go at it. An hour or so went by, and I headed home. While crossing the street, I noticed a black 1979 Chevy Monte Carlo roll by slowly, going in the opposite direction. Three or four guys with no shirts stared hard at me from inside. I could see they were drinking forty ounces of Old English and cussing at everybody walking on the street. They stared at me and I stared back. This pissed them off, and the chase was on.

The car gunned and swerved around leaving a black melted rubber C in the street. I started to run like a hunted deer. I didn't know them, and I didn't know what they wanted, but whatever it was I wanted no part of it. It was the early eighties, *Boyz in Da' Hood* and *Menace to Society* days, and young Black males were falling dead in the streets like raindrops in April. A look was all it took, wrong or not, to get killed. Like a virus, fratricidal proclivities were contagious, and to be infected it seemed you only needed to walk out of your front door. We fought a lot over nothingness. Gunplay was rampant, and the predator/prey game was all that was going on. One summer there were two or three shootings a day; half ended up dead, others paralyzed, while a few that survived wore their gunshot wounds like badges.

I dodged through the alley and single-hopped fence after fence, doubling back, thinking I could lose them. I could hear the roar of the engine but couldn't see them; I was running so fast everything was a blur: houses, lawns, cars, kids in the streets—everything blended in. They were predators, and they were locked in on me.

I didn't want to make a straight line home because I didn't want them to know where I lived, so I looped around several blocks and then hid between two houses, crouching down until I thought they'd given up. I sat there between the two houses sweating profusely and listening. It's surprising all of the things you can hear when you're afraid. The buzz of every insect, the movement of every tree, changes in the wind; your ears seem to revolve around your head like radar.

A few minutes went by and my heart rate had returned to normal. I started to move, planning my route home. I thought I was only a few blocks away, but somehow I'd gotten twisted around and soon realized I was a long way from home. I knew getting there was going to be like walking through a minefield. I eased out and began to make my way down the alley and into the streets. I began to pick up my pace when suddenly I looked up and saw directly across the street from me—the black Monte Carlo and three guys sitting on top of it. I froze. I couldn't and didn't run. It was as if they knew I would exit out that way. They came across the street laughing; one of them I could clearly see had a gun, a polished, snub-nose .38. A shield of calm washed over me, and I surrendered to an ill fate.

"You not running now," one of them said in a dense, bear-like growl.

"Why should I?" I asked defiantly.

"Why did you run before?"

"Why do you think? I don't know you, and you were chasing me."

"Yeah, that's right, you don't know us."

Never once did I look at the gun. I knew it was there, but there was no need to focus on it and then get broadsided in the jaw by not looking up. I stared ahead and became rigid. As they jawed at me and at each other, I listened, not saying a word. They teased me about my clothes, the colors, and asked about my gang affiliation. I didn't speak; I simply stared straight at them, waiting for the actual move that would get somebody hurt or dead.

As boys I think we sometimes feel it's easier to swallow a bullet than our pride. Little beads of sweat salted my pride to taste, and I swallowed quietly. From the corner of my eye, I saw the gun rise, but I never turned my head. My eyes squinted, my fists firmed, and my glare became more intense.

"You not scared now?" I was asked.

"Hell yeah, I'm scared, but what can I do about it now," I said as cool as I could, almost matter-of-fact. "I'm coming from playing baseball. I don't want anything from you, and you can't get anything from me. So what's the point?"

"The point is that I'm about to bust a cap in your dome and watch you fall. That's the point," said the gun-holder, and he pressed it forward against my right temple.

Whatever coolness steel has warms fast against flesh boiling in fear. Forging on the street, the pounding, the pressure, the heat, you either fall apart or take shape. Whatever was inside of me then was being revealed: no scraps.

The gun pressed against my head, but I didn't blink an eye. I dared not.

"You not scared, are you?" asked the head guy.

I shook my head no.

The big talker pushed the gun down and told them to let me go.

We all walked away. It was if it never happened. As if a page turned somewhere and we were expected to read on, slipping over the messiness of words with no meaning, moving the tragic story along.

They headed back across the street, and I made way toward home. It wasn't until I was a full block away that I started to run. I didn't stop until I reached the gravel of our driveway. My stepfather was in the garage and I ran inside. Tears, sweat, and dust had mixed to make a pasty mask on my face. He immediately knew something bad had happened because it took a lot for me to cry. He stared at me then lifted my head at the chin. His face was expressionless, but loud. Without asking what had happened, he told me to sit down on a chair just outside the garage door and think about what had happened and where I went wrong. He thought I had gotten beat up. I didn't talk about the gun because I knew he would grab his and then nothing would be good after that. It was the first time I heard him say, "There's no such thing as mistakes, son, just lessons about what not to do next time."

I understood that the implications far outweighed the thugs, and that there was something unreal, maybe even metaphorical, about what had just happened. I had to dig for it, but from that moment on I wasn't afraid of anything. When something like that happens, you put on a boldness that can at times be quite false, a façade to hide the damage done.

I sneaked out of the house a few mornings after the incident and ran down the creek looking to get to Mr. Gandy's house. He was coming up the back side, lugging fish, thick muddy clay about his bare feet. I was late. Before I got on the porch, he laughed. "I saw your dad, and he told me you got beat up."

"No, I didn't get beat up," I said. "I had a gun pulled on me."

"Is that right?" he asked nonchalantly. He leaned back, spread out some old newspaper, and laughed. "Well, the first time that happened to me was over an evil women and two dollars. How do you feel?"

I hadn't really thought about how I felt. I didn't know to actually plug into my "feelings." I just felt like I had to accept it, keep a keener eye, and move on.

Mr. Gandy could see the question left me wondering, staring out into space. Unhooking the fish and tapping open his blade, he said, "Yeah, son, it happens to men." Then he paused, froze stiff, dropped the fish, and leaned back in his chair. Still holding his knife, he slowly reached into his shirt pocket and pulled out a weathered leather tobacco pouch with a picture of a Black Indian stitched on the face. He pulled the drawstring, took two pinches of tobacco, and stuffed them deep and hard in his jaw. Closing the pouch and staring off into the same space, he said, "I can still hear those boys sometimes, pounding that steel, thumping the ground." He closed his eyes and bathed in the memory, his right foot tapping to a once lost beat, and then in a husky breath he let out a big "HUH."

With hands like sledgehammers he slapped me in the back of the head, and we laughed. Putting the pouch back in his pocket, he repeated with a big smile, "Yeah, son, it happens to men. Let's clean these fish so I can eat."

It took some time and many mistakes afterwards to realize I was damaged that day I had the gun in my face. It wouldn't be the last time I would be that close to meaningless violence or death. As boys we hide the scars, the imperfections in our metal, regardless of whether we're cast or forged.

Despite being forged metal reformed by fire, there was an anger I couldn't release, a fear I couldn't bury. It seemed everything became fragile and hard at the same time. There was nothing I could really embrace, and there was nothing I could really let go of. I held onto everything tightly, but at a distance. I was pounded and squeezed into something that day. It was the first of many foundries I'd enter in life.

Over the years I've given much thought to what we talked about a lot and still do. I'd only see Mr. Gandy a few more times after that. He died just as the frost was regularly dusting the ground that year. There but for a moment, our moment. A forged rail he helped set straight.

A BROKEN BEAM

Sometimes we lose faith in God, family, close friends, teachers, neighbors, mentors, and most importantly ourselves. We lose faith in seeing and striving for success. We lose faith in working toward great things—in having a sense of purpose. It can happen very quickly, or it can take some time. When such misfortune of the spirit falls, it can crush you from the inside out. It doesn't matter how strong you think you are; should you lose faith, things can unravel rather quickly.

I have had a number of reasons to lose faith. As a young man, you want a lot of things. You desire the latest games, clothes, and other material possessions that often your friends or others have. You can become so obsessed with acquiring "things" that you lose yourself and at times make very poor decisions in order to have what you want. Or you can become dismayed by witnessing the pain of others around you. I've witnessed many terrible things. I've seen those I loved and those I hardly knew abused and neglected. I've seen children in my neighborhood go hungry, live in dangerous homes, and at times become so distressed that they inflicted harm on themselves, or worst yet began to reproduce the pain.

As a kid I was strong, athletic, and smart in school. I had many friends. Each had his own problems at home, so whenever we got together the last thing any of us wanted to talk about was home. Everyone would talk about his dreams of doing this or doing that, and about leaving East St. Louis. For some the path was the military, for others basketball, football, or some kind of hustle. We didn't reach for each other's pains in any way. We dodged them and asked in unspoken words that they not be uttered. I think for boys, the ears and heart really can't take the pounding.

At this time in my life I could no longer see things clearly. I didn't know which way I was going. I couldn't voice the hurt I felt or speak to my own fears because I often found myself helping others deal with or solve their problems. I'm sure there were others around me who could see what was happening and became concerned. I am certain that they reached out to me and tried to help. But when you are wrapped in your own grief and self-loathing, you don't seem to be able to hear what others are saying to help you. I couldn't hear anybody, or maybe I simply refused help, which is easy to do when you don't know what it looks like.

I personally endured years of physical and mental abuse. As I was entering my teens, I felt life had become so rotten and dark in my eyes that I lost faith in everything around me. I sulked and brooded constantly. I sat in my room and

refused to talk. For some time I would leave
home in the mornings, walk to the park or an
open field, and sit all day allowing all of the
problems in my world to envelope me.

Early one spring morning, the weight of
my worries became so heavy, so unbearable, that I
tried to hang myself in the attic. I tossed a rope
across a beam, tied a noose, and stood on a chair.
After pulling the rope tight against my neck and
shedding a few tears, I leapt from the chair. I
swung, arms flailing away, reaching, grabbing, and
slipping.

In the coming darkness I heard a
tambourine. A burning rush whisked me away and
I found myself in the storefront church I attended
in Chicago. It was just as I remembered, a small
patchwork sanctuary flooded by the pastor's
baritone Pentecostal cadence replete with the
energy of the Holy Spirit, parishioners speaking
in tongue, dancing, fainting, fanning, and being
moved to rapture by an aged Hammond B3 and
the fiery syncopated clangs of the trap drum set's
ride cymbal and hi-hat. My grandmother handed
me a tambourine, her face glistening with sweat.
We were standing in the back of the church,
which was the front entrance. It was near a tiny
window where after church you could purchase
snow cones, candy, and other goodies.

"Play, baby," she said, smiling from ear
to ear, "walk with Christ."

I held the tambourine feeling heavy, feeling shame, my feet and hands unable to catch the beat. And I stood hearing, feeling, wishing, and wanting it to be real, wanting to take the walk. Nothing swayed me. I simply could not move. It got dimmer, the music began to fade, and the pulse began to wane. I could no longer see my grandmother but could hear her call, "Play, baby, play."

With a slight swing of my arm, the tambourine shook. I shook it again, then again, each time the vibrancy of the music and liveliness of the church moved closer and closer. I kept shaking then tapping its skin with the palm of my hand. The music got louder and louder, with shouting and "Hallelujahs" pouring over me. Slowly I found the beat until a feverous pitch and spiritual crescendo tugged, tugged and tugged at me, yanking me down to the floor figuratively and literally.

When you do something as foolish as I did, your mind immediately floods with regret. You forget what it was meant to solve. More times than not, you can't take back such actions. They are most always final. The beam that I'd tied the rope to snapped, and I fell to the floor. There was no one around to reverse the course had the beam not broken. I sat on the floor, looked up at the beam, and felt for what seemed like the first time the warmth of the morning sun, still hearing the tambourine. I loosened the noose, leaned against the wall, and let the rising day wash

over me, taking with it all my fears and worries.
The will to live again erupted inside me like a
volcano. It took the fear of death for me to
appreciate life.

A Black boy swinging from a rope—
Strange Fruit—stirs a great deal of grief for
potential loss to demons lurking in the dark.

I won't say things got easier, but they
seemed less difficult to cope with. To help
myself, I recalled a prayer in a birthday card
received from Chicago after my first year away. It
is called the Serenity Prayer[i]:

> God grant me the serenity
> to accept the things I cannot change,
> courage to change the things I can,
> and wisdom to know the difference.
>
> Living one day at a time,
> Enjoying one moment at a time,
> Accepting hardships as the pathway to
> peace, Taking, as He did, this sinful
> world as it is, not as I would have it,
> Trusting that He will make all things
> right if I surrender to His Will.

I memorized that prayer and found a way
to make it my own. I've leaned on it so often
you'd think I'd tire of it. But I never tire because
its words are refreshed with each challenge of
each day.

I was able to hide the broken beam, and I burned the rope. For years I never discussed my suicide attempt with anyone. In fact, I was well into my twenties before I ever uttered a word about the attempt and what I was feeling at the time. Knowing me as an adult, most people are shocked with disbelief when I bring it up. Sometimes I'm not sure whether it's because I've chosen to discuss it as a testimony of lost faith or because of the now-cracked perception of my inner strength. We all crack and peel in front and behind. It's the next step that matters. I've learned that a noose dangles near many times, and unwitting steps can lead us to swing.

At first I thought I was alone. Black boys don't commit suicide, so I thought. However, over time I realized that many young men who are hurting, confused, and faithless, as I was, have attempted suicide in one form or another. I've come to know young men who have tried to commit suicide through alcohol abuse or drug overdose. Others have tried through senseless violence, gun- or knife-play. There have been a few who were so determined to go to prison or jail with the expectation that someone there would do them harm. I once visited a young man in a hospital who'd been nearly fatally shot in a shoot-out with rival gang members within in one week of joining a gang. As we talked he revealed that what he was really trying to do was "go out blazing." He wanted to kill himself in a hail of bullets.

Many young men are not as fortunate as me or the young man in the hospital. Suicide among young Black men is more common than we think. It's a hushed tragedy. Some Black folk call it being "double-damned." Being damned once because you were born Black and male, a peculiar oddity to be loved, envied, feared, and loathed in America. Then being damned again because you squandered the blessing of life, held your grace too tight; your mind slumped and spirit crashed heavy, and you did the one thing God won't forgive. But funny how God will allow you to damn near hang yourself, then in Grace give you the break you need, the reprieve to try it again.

Depression, an emotional state with no boundaries, is serious. I always encourage young men who feel depressed or hopeless or as if the desire for self-harm has crept into their mind to seek help right away. I try to convince them they are not weak. To the contrary, bravery is facing what ails you. I share, almost reluctantly, my own fears, and state that even as a man you have to be courageous when you're weak, down, and battling mistakes. We live in a world that, should it see you burdened and kneeled by the weight of the yoke, will seek to take advantage, beat you while you're down, instill doubt, and question the purpose of your will to stand.

After I survived my attempt, I worked hard to never journey down that road again. It is literally a dead end. I got more focused in school, participated in sports; I even got an after-school job. I kept myself busy. I also began to listen to those who loved me and opened up to support and encouragement from teachers, coaches, and some neighbors. I started to volunteer, even becoming a Big Brother. What I began to learn is that when you help others, your life is enriched, and you value it more, because you realize that others value having you around—less for what you offer, and more for the spirit within. There's richness in vulnerability, in giving and learning each day to sacrifice some part of who you are. I once heard that service is the rent we pay for living. Pay often, and be sheltered.

Standing across the banks, you see the icy tide that gives rise to suicide. Grist to the mill are pitfalls and challenges, but beams don't always break, and you can't go back. You either rise from coarse earth or are ground down to nothing. Grasp your tambourine, young man, feel the shouts and Hallelujahs pouring over you, and "Play, baby, play."

PATHFINDER

How do you go about finding your path, the road to take, and your own pace? I must say that there are no secret formulas, at least none that I can recall. There are no magic wands to wave. What I am quite sure of is that moving forward is the only way you'll make the discovery.

You can be most certain that your intended path may not be where you think—the path that you eventually end up walking. Asking questions, some repeated, scouring under deadwood, and sifting through ashes for readymade answers is all a part of it. Some quiver at the notion of venturing forward toward some unclear or unknown destination. As young men we anxiously push forward with the impregnable breeze of fate as a tailwind.

As children we learned to survive by being creative—making a way out of no way, finding what fit, and making it work. We learned to make things, things that once seen or once touched moved ourselves and others to a better place than we were before. Creativity lent beauty to the monotony of everyday existence.

I do pity most young men today in part
for this reason: most don't know how to make
much. The market has made things cheap and
accessible, but not very durable. You learn how to
use then dispose. There's no part of you in what
you handle day to day. It becomes easy, then, to
disregard and discard. Every young man should
tinker with wood and metal, even clay. You
should learn to change a tire, change oil, hang a
door, carve with a chisel, use sandpaper, and paint
with a brush. Learn to use a screwdriver, a
wrench, and other kinds of tools from all kinds of
crafts. The point is that you learn to use your
hands, make them nimble and an extension of
your ideas and abilities.

Many of the toys we played with we had
to make. We did this from whatever we could
scrounge up or from whatever lay around our
back yards and alleys, or even in the junk that
dotted the streets. There was no money to visit a
bike shop, stroll through, and find a shiny new
two-wheeler in the most perfect color. As boys we
loved to ride our bikes. Sometime we'd fly down
an alley sparkling with broken glass, shards of
wood, and twisted rusted metal. We'd race trains
head-on at nearby tracks, bobbing violently on
the rail ties and jumping off a short hill a few
moments shy of becoming bug splatter on the
front end of a locomotive. Our favorite love,
though, was to careen brakeless down the rough
side of a great hill that had about as much slope
as the top of a silo. Miniature-sized boulders,
roots, and sinkholes speckled the ride down. It

took skill and sheer nerve because once you let go from the top there was no stopping, pausing, or time-out until you hit the bottom, on or off the bike. I'm sure this helped foster my love for mountain biking and mountain climbing today. Conquering a hill can bring a sense of sheer freedom. However, this is a tenuous and brief sensation because hills and mountains are unconquerable, success is temporary, and for this you feel reverence.

Whenever the brothers and I were ready to ride a hill, we needed a master ramp-builder. There were only a handful around, and I prided myself on being one of them. Perhaps my love of science and math fed my desire to build things. To this day my aunt Mildred loves to tell the story of seeing me build a "store" out of pieces of plywood one summer where I sold candy, gum, and other goodies to the kids in the neighborhood. I was eleven or twelve at the time. It was the first time I fired someone. My friend Marcus, who wanted to be part owner and share in the profits, wouldn't help gather wood, drill, drive a nail, or screw, and sometimes wouldn't show up at all to help.

After being gone for about two days, he showed up at the site near my house and the "store" was completely built and I had already started making sales. He wanted to work for me behind the counter, and when I refused he asked if he could help advertise the store by riding his bike through the neighborhood telling all the kids about it. I had already paid another kid in the neighborhood five dollars to do this. He became upset, mounted his bike, and rode away. We didn't play or ride together much after that.

Had I waited on Marcus I would have probably missed the bulk if not the entire summer of candy sales. So I did it myself. I'm not sure what Marcus ended up with that summer but I suspect not much because he didn't want to work for anything. I on the other hand made enough money to buy my school clothes, and a few things for my siblings at the end of the summer.

My friends and I could build ramps that would launch us into the stratosphere. Bike after bike would pound the front end of a ramp constructed of scraps of wood so solid an Army Corps Engineer would envy it. Our ramps wouldn't wobble, and they could be moved from location to location and be used over and over. I'd like to think that one or two of them remain covered in some overgrown weeds near some stream or in the back yard of one of the abandoned homes in East St. Louis. I'd also like to believe that they could be dusted off and still set to go at the bottom of some enticing hill someday. That's the point, though. You want to believe that the things you make can last. Something crafted from your hands, drawn from the surfaces of your mind, can be left behind and covered by neglect or natural forces beyond your control, but once reclaimed can still mean something to someone.

Thinking back, brothers hurt themselves coming down hill after hill. Many bumps and bruises, sprained and broken limbs, were had for the thrill of trying to see how high we could fly. There was a strengthening amongst us to know that from scraps of metal we could craft a bike without brakes, nothing to slow us down or to lean our fears on, something strong that would not break down on us as we sped forward. And there was a joyful pride amongst the craftsmen to know that for those brothers who made it through the rough-and-tumble downhill trial, awaiting them was a launching point. One built of our own hands, and where in our minds we helped each other reach new heights.

***

"What kind of man are you?" my uncle Otha often asked with the intensity of a jackhammer. Quite often I would have no answer. I had never dared ask the question of myself.

All of my uncles, including my uncle Otha, are Black man cut from a unique and richly textured cloth. Having to cut through the thickets and weeds of racism, Black self-loathing, and segregation to reach clear fields has left them marked in some subtle and not-so-subtle ways. When you look in their eyes, you can see that the journey wasn't easy, that sometimes success was sweet and sometimes bitter, and that thorns can leave deep scars. At times they'll pick up a worn sickle for old time's sake in search of a familiar grip, just in case.

My uncle Otha's question would return time and time again until I had an answer.

The first time he asked me the question I had just started college, wide-eyed and to an extent full of pride. I was eager to be at the University of Illinois, one of the best schools in the country. I had made it to Champaign, Illinois, from very humbling and at times painful circumstances. East St. Louis, where I completed my high school education, has been described as America's Soweto.

In the late eighties and early nineties, East St. Louis was famous for the excellence youth showed on the field, the brutality showed to one another, and the apathy local and state leadership showed to the world. I'm not sure if it was hunger, the bad rashes people would get from the water when the rains fell hard, the dilapidated housing, unemployment, or the leaded soot you felt under your feet when you walked barefoot in the dirt. Whatever it was, it made people want to fight—sadly, though, it was a need to fight each other. Ravaged souls can devour one another, and in "East Boogey," the feeding was plenty.

East St. Louis Senior High School had the number one football team in the country, winning three straight state titles. East St. Louis had produced several prominent athletes in track

and field, basketball and football, including
Olympians Al Joyner and Jackie Joyner-Kersee.
East St. Louis Lincoln High School, the other
high school in town, had the nation's number-one
jazz band and high school basketball team. Both
high school scholastic teams were the first all
African-American teams from the area to compete
in statewide and national scholastic bowls with
tremendous success, and produced young people
that competed nationally for math and science
awards.

This success was often shaded dark and
tragic, however, by other events in East St. Louis.
The author Jonathan Kozol featured East St.
Louis in his book *Savage Inequalities*. I still
remember his visit to our high school, which
Kozol wrote about in his book:

"Anyone who visits in the schools of
East St. Louis, even for a short time, comes away
profoundly shaken. These are innocent children,
after all. They have done nothing wrong. They
have committed no crime. They are too young to
have offended us in any way at all. One searches
for some way to understand why a society as rich
and, frequently, as generous as ours would leave
these children in their penury and squalor for so
long—and with so little public indignation. Is
this just a strange mistake of history? Is it
unusual? Is it an American anomaly?"

Quoted in the book was a fourteen-year-
old girl who stated, "We have a school...named

for Dr. King…. The school is full of sewer water and the doors are locked with chains. Every student in that school is Black. It's like a terrible joke on history."

Martin Luther King Jr. Junior High School, the school I attended, is no longer there.

Our lives along the Mississippi were contorted by a mix of pride and devastation. East St. Louis still often ranks first in the state in fetal death and in premature birth. The harshest memories I have, though, are the violence. I was a young man of an age when violence stalked you, lingered around your mornings and slept at the edges of your night. You never knew when or how close it would come to you.

Once while attending the aforementioned ML King Jr. Junior High School, I watched a young man be stabbed in the neck with an ice pick by his best friend, a guy who wanted his spot in the gang to which they both belonged. What was most shocking to me at the time was how unaffected the adults were. There was no urgency to get him help. Among young people there was no urgency to flee the scene. You could hear him utter words in a soft whisper. He'd come to God at that moment. This told me he knew better but had refused to do better, like many of us. He'd always known God existed and assumed He'd always be there—to ease the transition. Each whisper was a plea that God would be. Like the wilting of a tulip, his death was no big deal. That

is what tulips do: bloom for a short time, then
fade. It was his time to fade, and surely tomorrow
it would be someone else's.

Ironically, the mayor's family owned the
largest funeral home in town. The running joke
was that he had a conflict of interest. Dead
babies, school violence, poor health, and horrific
environmental conditions were all good for
business.

Some of those who gave me a leg up
barely had a leg to stand on. They were hustlers,
thieves, and men who, given the opportunity,
would have been great in a number of ways. Many
had survived Jim Crow, barely. They were scarred
and angry, and had surrendered to play the deck
they were handed. The one key difference I
believe between then and now is that they wanted
something better for you, and would make damn
sure you knew it.

Every day someone would try to impart
pieces of their dreams in you; advice would come
from my elders, older Black men, who in their
quiet invisibility passed on many valuable lessons.
They were invisible because they went day to day
making what they could out of nothing. They
were caring, responsible, and above all consistent.
Yes, they were imperfect. Many were broken, and
therefore human. None, as I can recall, were
shattered, and they were therefore men.

They fought for our voices, for small freedoms, for the opportunity to be an example. They weren't respected for it because it often didn't pay well. I'm speaking of teachers, mechanics, junk men, sanitation workers, bus drivers, gas station attendants, grocery clerks, butchers, tailors, handy men, factory workers, and carpenters. Like most endangered species, they became extinct because of the natural and unnatural order of things.

I learned from them that there is an art to taking others' success personally. Being conscious that what you create allows others to pursue their days and get done, or even just through, what is before them.

Among them, I was often called "Little Professor" and asked to read the newspaper or spark up discussion on some current event, which would start a good, heated debate about economics, politics, family, community, and everyday society. So my first lecture halls were pool halls, barber shops, junkyards, garages, lounges, "juke joints," and sitting under shade trees in vacant lots. I learned to speak, mocking the smooth verbal cadence of the preachers and wordsmiths that frequented these places.

When I first received my letter of acceptance into the University of Illinois, I shared it with these men, one of whom was my stepfather, who had a sixth-grade education. What erupted in these men couldn't be called pride. Pride was too small of a measure. It was an emotion about turning the page, moving the story forward. It is an emotion I still carry.

***

You don't reach great heights alone. Some blaze ahead and carve out the trail before you, while others solidly build a point from which you can launch.

Another influential person early in my life didn't come from the streets. She was my high school counselor, Mrs. Ledora A. Williams, whom we called "the Law" because her initials spelled LAW. She was hard on students, and it was the most real love many of us ever had. She elevated expectations and took it personally if you failed.

One day after getting in some trouble, I was sitting in the assistant principal's office awaiting my paddling. They paddled then with quarter-inch–thick leather straps, and they didn't miss the mark.

The Law happened to come by and ask me what I was doing there. I told her what I'd done, and after talking more with me she gave me the most peculiar look. "You don't talk like a fool," she said. "What junior high did you attend?" "King," I answered. "Come with me," she said. She told the assistant principal she was taking me, and he didn't put up a fuss. I don't think he wanted to paddle me anyway. I had been sitting there through two class periods. We went into her office and she pulled up my file, thumbing through the pages and pausing to huff when something interesting caught her attention. She peered over her glasses with the fiercest of looks. At that point the paddling didn't seem like a bad option.

"You're too smart to be this stupid," she fussed, as only the Law could, with the fierceness of a lioness protecting her young. And that's how she made you feel, protected. In all of the chaos of the day to day, Mrs. Williams looked out for your well-being, even if at the time you resisted it because you didn't know any better. "I'm putting you in our Principal Scholars Program to see if we can't get you straightened out." There was no debate—I think because I wanted to be straightened out. Sometimes we scream in silence to be saved, and it's the caring heart that tunes in the sound. The Law raised expectations for me and subsequently of me. Sometimes that's all it takes, a bar to be set—something to focus on. Sometimes it takes more.

Taskmasters like Mrs. Mays, my English teacher, who insisted we digest Shakespeare, Hawthorn, Chaucer, Tolstoy, Orwell, Wright, and others in a rich literary canon, intended to prepare us for college. She graded our papers with a ruler to check the margins and that each line was level. This was before word processors; we used typewriters and were penalized for sloppy typing. We mastered the art of handwriting and then typing because paper was expensive and we were not allowed to use white-out. And we loved Mrs. Mays for it. To this day I handwrite everything before typing a word.

Our math and science teachers insisted on excellence and made us feel that in their classrooms there was no such thing as average. We took this sense of worth with us, wore it around our necks like a warm scarf in the harshness we knew we'd face once we left the building and crossed the street into the real world.

I took being a Principal Scholar serious. It made me feel I was responsible for something other than myself. Teachers looked at you differently; you didn't need a hall pass and were taken at your word most times. I mean, you were given trust on a tray decorated with doilies and populated with delicate hopes to carry forward, and you didn't want to mess anything up. Adults had marked and approved you as someone who was going somewhere and did what they could to move some hurdles out of your way so you could learn to overcome the rest in stride.

The idea of a village was alive on many occasions. From the cooks in the cafeteria who kept extra plates so you could come back and get more because they knew you'd be staying after school or taking some home, to the janitor who unlocked the side doors that led away from the fights, teasing, and doom. From the barber who would cut your hair for free if you had no money but had to compete in a Scholar Bowl, because it made him proud, to the city bus driver who didn't punch your bus pass as long as you sat up front and talked baseball, Negro league. Somebody somewhere gave you a little extra nudge to get by and get along. If you had something to say, you were heard. That is, if you were in need and could voice it, and it was serious and you were sincere, you were heard. Sometimes it could take a little while for somebody to respond or make sense of what you were going through. But once they got it, they would extend themselves, so you learned patience and to be appreciative of whatever you received.

The idea of going to college started to build and I fully embraced it. We started making trips to Champaign-Urbana as a part of Principal Scholars and Upward Bound, we met the counselors and graduates of our high school would play host. I was so excited about the possibility of college, of learning, of exploring. All I needed to do was keep my eyes forward, my head down, and my hands on the plow, and I would make it.

We were prepared to arrive on any college campus ready to compete. For the most part, many of us were academically ready. Intellect may help you rise from the squalor and swamp of poverty and depravity, but bits tend to stick, blemish, and stain. Some of the filth never washes

off, no matter how hard you scrub. The biggest
deficiency from growing up poor is deprivation of
self-image. There are those who succumb, and
their damage is readily seen—while others, the
scramblers and high achievers, work to conceal
the damage through insatiable pursuits of reward
and recognition. Many heal, but it's a pitiful
burden of circumstance.

"There are three kinds of men in this
world," my uncle Otha said once. "There are
those who make things happen, those who watch
things happen, and those who don't know what in
the hell is happening. Which one are you?"

I struggled to answer him. It took some
time for me to even get it. After many failures and
struggles with the question and what it really
meant, I had to pick one. Reflecting on my days
in East St. Louis, my own hunger, my own scars,
and the ghosts I see from time to time have made
me realize that if I weren't a man who would
make things happen, I'd better learn how to
become one. And that is how I started on my
path.

FEAR, THE TERRIBLE THIEF

Fear is a terrible thief. It robs, maims, and strips the spirit. Fear can hold you in a grip so tight that the need to breathe takes precedent over the desire to move.

Momma West and my aunt Blanche came to East St. Louis to attend my high school graduation and to bring me back to Chicago. It had been nine years since I left. I was bound for Champaign-Urbana, about 130 miles south of Chicago, but wanted to reconnect, to re-root myself, and going home was good.

I had a full academic scholarship as I entered the College of Agricultural Sciences. My plan was to major in agricultural economics then pursue an MBA. At the time I wanted to trade commodities. I had dreams of making millions trading soybeans, sugar, cattle futures, pork bellies, coffee, and metals. It didn't happen that way. I had a very raggedy start. It took a while for me to realize that I was still in a sense beat up, lost, and confused. While I had worked hard to get myself into the University of Illinois (U of I), I hadn't worked hard enough on myself. Mostly because I didn't know I had to, and had I known I wouldn't have known where to start. I also had

many fears upon entering the U of I, and after all
it took for me to get there, I flunked out in my
first semester.

The U of I has over thirty thousand
undergraduate students, an enormous campus,
two college towns, and lots to do that has nothing
to do with academics. Poor studying and social
habits dragged behind me when I left East St.
Louis. There were also remnants of self-loathing,
self-doubt, and anger from prejudice. The first
series of required courses during freshman year
are taken in cavernous auditoriums. Black
students on campus liked to say we were "flies in
the buttermilk" because of the specks of Black
faces in a sea of White ones. For me it was very
intimidating. It wasn't like I hadn't had any
interaction with young Whites, but my
experiences were few and far in-between, and not
very pleasant. East St. Louis is surrounded by
several predominantly White communities where
as a child you dared not venture for fear of being
harassed, stopped by police, or physically harmed.
We would hear stories of mobs of young White
boys whose job it seemed was to patrol their
neighborhoods for strays.

Whenever we traveled to any
predominantly White community for athletic and
academic competitions, we were told to stay
together, stay close, and be aware at all times of
our surroundings. We were awed by the awesome,
meticulously landscaped high school campuses,
with operable swimming pools, spotless cafeterias

and hallways, and libraries the size of our gym that had rich woods tables, comfortable chairs, bright lighting, computers, typewriters, and what appeared to us to be more than fifty times the number of books we had.

We also lost most of our academic matches with White high schools. This isn't to say we weren't competitive. There were occasions we'd win matches and be filled with tremendous pride. Our losses, however, taught me that they had an edge. Truth be told, it was an advantaged that lingered in the mind of every high-achieving Black student I knew. It was a harsh and sometimes intense realization that while we were in the top five or ten percent of our high school graduating class, we'd actually be in the top twenty or twenty-five percent of most any White high school's class. Several of the Black students that graduated in the top of their high school class didn't make it beyond freshman or sophomore year at their respective colleges and universities.

The pressure to be a shining example of your community and the weight of family, church, or school expectations was overwhelming for a number of top Black students. Many were the first in their family or community to go to college, to leave home to advance their education, or attend a predominantly White university. There were whispers of suicide attempts, drug abuse and overdose, and complete mental breakdowns.

Entering U of I, the veneer of achievement was pulled back; I was exposed and felt grossly inadequate and afraid. It was like always having to ask for permission to be at the U of I. There was an air of ownership among White students, and for me and a number of other Black students, it felt like we were trespassing. We struggled as Black students to find our own space, some corner of the campus community where we could establish our own identities, where we could reinforce and reassure one another. Fraternities, sororities, social clubs, dance groups, tiny study groups, and weekly parties helped us with creating our own rites and rituals for success, and for failure.

A 2.0 grade point average was required of freshman during the first semester. My grade point average in my first semester was far below this, and because I hadn't made satisfactory academic progress and was deemed "scholastically deficient," I was dismissed from the program and lost my scholarship. I was devastated.

I wasn't buying being "scholastically deficient" although I knew deep inside I had some deficiencies. I lacked focus and discipline, habits I did not develop early on. Up until that point I had relied on my natural abilities. I could read and comprehend quickly and loved science so it came easy; math wasn't difficult, and I could write. But when you have not learned or mastered how to put these abilities together consistently, it doesn't add up to much; they're just moving parts with no momentum and no purpose.

I was in my dorm room when I received the news that I was out of college. The future I thought I had evaporated. It was winter break, so I packed an old green army duffle bag and headed to the Greyhound station eight miles or so from the dorm, to go home. As I walked I reflected on what awaited me in Chicago. There was nothing there. North Lawndale isn't East St. Louis, but it's a close cousin. Being young, Black, male, jobless, and not in school was also a bad combination. By the time I reached the bus station I knew I couldn't leave campus. I had to get back in school.

I turned around and headed to Mumford Hall, the home of the College of Agriculture. The dean happened to be in. He agreed to meet with me and explained that it was academic policy; there was nothing he could do. He was very stern and detached, almost remote, leaning heavily on the language of bureaucracy and policy. I was completely defeated and resigned to some ill-fated outcome.

I couldn't leave, though. I hung around the college all day into the night. I spent the night there thinking, wondering about what was next and how badly I'd blown it.

Early the next day, I had given up. I planned to go back to Chicago, attend a community college, and start over. As I slung my duffle bag on my back, I heard a very familiar voice. It was Kandeh Yumkella, our graduate advisor. He looked at me in a peculiar fashion and asked me why I was standing there with that bag so early in the morning. I went on to explain my situation and that I wanted to stay and complete my studies. He asked if I had spoken with the dean. I said that I had.

He gave me a good tongue-lashing in his thick African accent, expressing how disappointed he was and how the world was full of bright young men who had wasted their abilities on foolishness. I was speechless. I stared at the floor. He told me to go back to my dorm room and wait for him to figure out what to do and if he could help. Before I left he said, "Joseph, you have too much to give the world. We have to figure this out."

I wasn't very hopeful, but I walked to my dorm room and stretched across the bed. I hadn't slept well the night before. My roommate, Marcus, walked in and was surprised to see me. He thought I was in Chicago. I told him what happened and that Kandeh said he would try to figure something out. Just saying that Kandeh was willing to help me made me feel worse because I knew there were so many people who had believed in me. Marcus said he would wait around with me.

I read a little and listened to music. At about midday Marcus suggested that we go and get lunch and maybe go shoot some ball rather than sit around. Playing basketball did take my mind off of my troubles for a moment. As we were leaving the gym and walked back to the dorm room, I began to really admire the beauty of the campus, the plenteousness of facilities, and really appreciate where I was for the first time. There was no sewer water, no bullets, and no thick, harsh air. I hadn't taken it in before. I thought this would be the last time I would see it, so I paused and breathed it all in.

When we got back to our room, I had a message from Kandeh on the answering machine. He sounded hesitant, but hopeful. He said he had spoken to the dean and that maybe, it wasn't definite, but maybe they could work something out. He said I should go home for the break and he would be in touch. I took that long journey home and waited. It was winter in Chicago, the coldest yet, it seemed. I didn't enjoy Christmas and made only one resolution for New Years.

"If given another chance, Lord...."

Halfway through the break I received word from Kandeh that there was a compromise to give me another chance. I didn't ask what the compromise was, and Kandeh didn't tell me. We both understood that whatever was offered was far better than me returning home—far better. Once again, I felt I'd dodged a bullet.

As it turned out, the agreement was that I would lose my scholarship, be placed on academic probation where I would have to get a 2.5 GPA or greater the following semester, remain on academic probation until I attended summer school, submit a study plan each semester, and meet with Kandeh on a more regular basis. Since I'd lost my scholarship, I would have to work. I took a job at the university's physical plant as a night custodian cleaning chalkboards, mopping floors, disposing of trash, and dusting halls. I had another chance, and I never gave in to fear again.

While squeezing out sea sponges, folding cheesecloth, and polishing desks sometime between midnight and 2:00 a.m., I asked myself what I really wanted. I appreciated the work, the humbling nature of it, but in all honesty this wasn't what I wanted, not what I'd left home for. I thought about those who had given me a hand up, who had lent their love, and how I was squandering it. I had to get serious or stop taking up space for someone else.

I became intensely focused and expanded my world. The following summer I became an orientation student leader (OSL) where I gave tours and lead groups for incoming freshman and their parents. Being an OSL really helped me appreciate the history, diversity, and resources of the U of I. I made a number of new friends, many of them White, and opened up my mind to new possibilities and experiences.

What clicked inside of me was the question of what would happen should I fail. What would I do or become should I be defeated? There was also a part of me that saw a deep well where there was nothing to grab a hold of to pull myself up or out. In the bottom of that well were the many faces of lost potential, especially young men with aspirations to be engineers, doctors, teachers, something other or more than what they had become used to seeing. For those who could not see something different in their homes or neighborhoods, in themselves, that part of their vision died. I didn't want that to be me. To keep me focused and on task, I sought help. I spoke with my academic counselor, reworked my plan to graduate, changed my major, got a tutor, and began eliminating distractions. Once I had something better before me to reach out and grab a hold of, I let go of fear and refused to be robbed.

I even spent some time with a therapist. Like all toxic waste, bad memories need a safe place for proper disposal. I learned you can't figure it all out on your own. You really don't know what's buried inside until it starts to roll off your tongue like peeling tar. I was using both hands to pull out of me the anger, disgust, and discontent until it no longer hurt to breathe, and even love myself and others deeply.

I became more comfortable with myself. I learned to serve by volunteering for prison

literacy program and working at the Boys and
Girls Club. By the time I graduated, my peers
selected me to deliver our graduation speech.
Kandeh Yumkella completed his Ph.D. and went
on to have many outstanding accomplishments,
including becoming the Director-General of the
United Nations Industrial Development
Organization (UNIDO). I completed my studies
at the University of Illinois, worked for a while in
Chicago as a social worker and public health
researcher, and then went on to Harvard School
of Public Health where I earned both master's
and doctorate degrees.

Some get it right, while others never will.
To me that's hell. Never being able to get it right
and repeating the same mistakes, causing the same
confusion and living off the same grief over and
over. Some days you will fail miserably—your
dap won't matter, your hustle won't flow, and
every thought will simply be a weight added onto
the thoughts that preceded it. Your life can lie in
the balance—when the next turn you take could
well be your last. And it is moments such as these
when you must hold on, dig deep, and be
courageous.

A STUCK HOG'S SCREAM

Have you ever heard a stuck hog scream? It's a final appeal stirred with the trepidation of impending death and the burning slip of fading hope for a savior from the slaughter. It's akin to a pleading mother, broken, as she watches her child taken away to prison. It's the sprawled-out girlfriend on the emergency room floor, peppered in blood and caught in a recurring tempest of "Why?" It's the father in the morgue staring at an image that looks just like him, only that figure has breathed half as much. It's the callous-palmed grandmother, teary-eyed and scraping together scriptures to toss behind a lost soul lingering between one world and the next, hoping one will stick and serve as a passport to heaven. It's the arrhythmic panting of being shattered and spread out, waiting for the axe to fall.

I've been there. In the slaughterhouse of a courtroom where young men are strung out, high, and gutted to the empty cries of loved ones crushed and tucked away in the corner. Too hurt to watch, but too caring to walk away.

At the cusp of one summer while I was working on my doctoral studies, my youngest brother carjacked, robbed, and executed a Marine

in a school playground. He then took the car and
the money and went to a party without the
slightest second thought. When I received the call
about his arrest and the sketchy details of what
he'd done, everything seemed to collapse upon
itself. His trial started the following year and he
was sentenced to a life sentence without parole
plus forty-two years. He was only seventeen years
old. Though guilt draped over him like an iron
blanket, his trial was a joke.

His defense attorney was poorly prepared
and stuttered horribly. Anyone who has ever seen
the movie *My Cousin Vinny* and is familiar with
the first defense attorney can get the picture. As
in the movie, the defense attorney strolled
through the courtroom enveloped in a false air of
confidence. That air burst when he opened his
mouth. It took him five minutes to clear one
sentence. After a few days of this, no one wanted
to listen anymore or be bothered by a trial. If the
judge and jury weren't going to sentence my
brother for the murder, they were going to
sentence him for having to sit through his
defense.

There was some verbal scuffling between
my siblings and I over exactly what he should be
defended against; the murder of another human
being, a marine and beloved son—another Black
man or his own death from suffocation due to the
violent suction of love from his life. It's easy to
point to the failure of adults in his life. It was
adults that failed to teach him to read. It was

adults that left a child wandering the streets in search of shelter, food and closeness. And it was an adult that used him then sent him off with a loaded "hand-cannon", angry, wounded and cold. Of course ultimately he was culpable. But I wonder. Where would he be had he'd been given just a little more sustenance? The sticky sweet kind coating his soul like dripping soft serve on a cone where he could have lapped it up in childlike delight.

I felt then, as I sometimes do now, that I had failed him, that I didn't pause enough from my own pursuits to really see his pain. There's still the lingering guilt of an older brother who failed to catch his younger brother as he fell. When he was but knee high to a duck I shared my food with him. I shared my bed with him. I can still recall him rolling up next to me at night afraid of what the darkness held. I even shared my clothes. But it seemed I could never share enough of myself. I'd filled my life with my own challenges, and it has chafed me that I hadn't pushed them aside long enough to help him deal with his.

My brother was only seven years old when his parents split for good. And to me he never recovered. He longed for his father. He longed to understand the distance and the jagged edges that remained. Neither his father nor his mother could explain it to him in a way that made sense or did him any good. Unfortunately he and my other siblings got the worst of his father, and

I got the best of him. He was called Hawk, short
for his last name Hawkins, but perhaps also
because you could always see the hunting in his
eyes. He'd been in and out of jail since he was
twelve years old. He had a sixth-grade education
and had been living on his own since before he
was a teenager.

Everyone in East St. Louis knew Hawk.
He couldn't be missed. He was six-foot-three,
about 250 pounds, and was prison-carved strong.
My brother was the spitting image of his father,
and our mother never let him forget it. Hawk was
first convicted of auto theft in 1962, and then in
1965 for running a chop shop. This was the
family business growing up in East St. Louis. It
was lucrative, and it was all my stepfather knew.
On any given day, the chop shop would clear
$1500 or more. Hawk was brilliant and exacting
in so many other ways that only I had a chance to
see. He could do math in his head or on the back
of a paper bag, calculating weights of metals and
prices, costs, and expenses all in a flash. No one
ever dared to cheat him.

He taught me the tenets of hard work.
Many days he'd wake me before the sun rose to
help him dismantle a car or load up a truck with
car parts before going to school. On the weekends
we would start cutting up a car at 3:00 a.m., have
the parts loaded by seven, arrive in Cape
Girardeau, Missouri, about 9:30 a.m. for
breakfast, unload the truck by noon, and be back

in time for me to play baseball or shoot hoops with my friends.

On those trips he'd emphasize the importance of knowing how to work with your hands. "In case you ever have to feed yourself or just make it," he'd say. But he also pressed the seriousness of going to school. Doing what we were doing wasn't a career option. It was what he knew, and it fed us, housed us, kept us warm in the winter, and allowed us to enjoy some of life's bigger crumbs. But I wasn't to think any more of it than that. And he meant it.

I started driving the truck at fifteen and could dismantle a Chevy, Buick, Cadillac, or Oldsmobile before going to school, except for the transmission. We never did Fords, Toyotas, or Hondas; the parts didn't sell well. Buyers only wanted GM, Mercedes, BMW, and high-end parts. Not that I ever had the desire, but I was never allowed to steal cars. Hawk felt that if caught it would destroy my chances of going to college. He also said that there was no real money in that work. So he'd pay others who had walked that path before, who'd spent time in jail, and for whom college was a myth. It taught me to rise early, put in a full day, and have the remainder of the day to do whatever you want, but never waste the meat of the day.

It taught me to see both sides of the truth. That the good guys aren't always good and the bad guys aren't always bad. It was a game of survival, and a number of police officers, politicians, businessmen, reputable car dealers, and body shop owners played. It was cheaper for a big car dealer or body shop to buy stolen parts to use for their repairs then to buy wholesale from the manufacturer. The markups on parts were huge. Sometimes parts would be slightly damaged or didn't work well from the start. It didn't matter, though. It made for repeat customers doing repeat repairs. The common man had no idea that when he had an accident and needed his car repaired, the parts for it might well have come from his neighbor's car that was stolen a week earlier.

Ironically, all of this served me well in college and at Harvard. Not everybody was clean, and not everybody played fair. There was different surveillance and enforcement for Blacks and Whites. And ideas, like cars, could be looted, stripped, and repackaged for resale.

The sellers were mostly Black, and the buyers were all White. It was the sellers who got caught the most, and the buyers never seemed to go out of business. Hawk did well not to get caught because he had White friends, and that gave him a pass many times. But one cool, crisp spring morning Hawk was arrested and whisked away to prison. State police troopers and FBI agents surrounded the house, guns drawn, kicking in doors, stalking the streets, and sealing off the block. News vans streamed images of dismantled automobiles and automobile parts that lay under tarps in our garage. Federal agents cleared out the garage in the back of our house, removing large wenches, blowtorches, gas tanks filled with oxygen and other gases, hundreds of pounds of tools, and other chop shop equipment. Police kicked holes in the walls looking for money. They stuffed bags of cash, of course not all of it, and papers into the trunks of their cars. News reporters knocked on neighbors' doors, peeked into our front window, and pointed at our house as they talked into microphones and cameras. Soon there was a small crowd of onlookers. The sun had barely shown the top of its head when the ordeal began to unfold.

I choose to walk through the chaos outside our door and go to school. I didn't lower my head or bury my face. When I got to school, people were talking about the news story, but I didn't answer questions and I didn't care what was said. To me it was business, and I had to take care of my own and stay in school. One of my teachers was a good friend of my stepfather and let me stay in his room all day that day. He owned one of the juke joints we hung in from time to time. We struggled for a long time after that.

While Hawk was in prison our family went on welfare. The crumbs became smaller, tasteless and harder to come by. It would be embarrassing to wait in line at the Armory for unnamed canned goods and a block of cheese, which we'd have to pay two dollars to have it

sliced at the local Kroger grocery store. My sister
and I were in the free-lunch line now during the
school year and in the summer, which I rarely ate
because I could hardly stomach the barren
selection.

After Hawk was released from Centralia
Correctional Center he couldn't make any moves
on the streets, not even legitimate ones. For
keeping quiet and not naming names he had a
sizable cut of cash waiting for him. But we were
so behind on bills and nearly naked in aged and
worn clothes the money didn't last long. He hated
being on welfare and I could see, even feel at
times, how it ate away at his dignity. There was
no time more poignant than when an unpleasant
rust color haired social worker showed up at our
front door one morning with the brutal authority
of an emboldened prejudice White woman.

She and other White women were
visiting the fields beating the bushes for Black
men, forcing them to scatter like rabbits. All the
homes were supposed to be vacated by Black men,
and Black women on welfare were supposed to be
burdened by a mass of unruly children, destitute
and love starved.

Hawk was home sitting in his chair when
the social worker pounded on the door with her
clipboard in hand. He ran into the basement
hiding in my room while we all dusted ourselves
off and lined up in the living room for inspection.
It was a sickening scramble. I choked on the

supercilious air the social worker dragged in as she, without asking, plopped down in the chair just warmed by the man of the house. Excusing formalities she began to gun questions at our mother about work and her social life. She asked about our school progress and in shrouded sincerity asked us about our friends and how often we visited other family. Then out came the lie, our lie. Straightening her back, gripping her ballpoint pen and leaning forward in a dare, she asked, "Have you seen your father? Does he live here?" We had to deny him. Deny he existed. Deny his presence, his command, his love. We had to look as pitiful and fatherless as we could. "No," we said in unison and stared at the floor knowing he was just below us, and I knew he could hear. Half satisfied with our performance the social worker left ensuring that the checks would keep coming as she walked out the door. There was perhaps no singular experience more than this one that solidified my drive to go to school. I'd never be the rabbit under the living room floor.

As the door closed behind the social worker I heard Hawk come up from the basement. He stood in the kitchen as if barricaded from the living room where we were still standing on display. He turned heavily and walked out the back door. Breaking ranks I went after him. I sat next to him wanting to say I was sorry, but knew I didn't have to. He pulled out a pack of Pall Mall cigarettes and thumped it twice on the back of his hand. He lit a square taking a

long draw. He thumbed a few ashes from the end
of the cigarette and said, 'son let me tell you
about the world in Black and White." He began
to talk, and I listened taking in all the cool of his
pain. Less than a week later he was back doing
what he knew how to do. And we didn't ever have
to stand in any line again, and deny him.

***

When I was a little boy in Oklahoma I
would watch my cousins and uncles slaughter
hogs. Hog slaughtering started the day before,
isolating the hog, not feeding it, flushing it with
water. Then the shotgun blast: and the hog broke
down to its knees. Quickly they'd roll it over,
slitting the throat just above the breastbone, but
gently so as not to make it bleed inside. A large,
boiling vat filled with water and vinegar or
sometimes corn liquor was prepared to scald the
hair from the carcass. The hog was lifeless as it
was handled from pen to vat. But when you
dropped it into the hot water, it came to life,
squealing, squirming, and making a deafening
scream. It was then hung upside down and
stripped with a bell scraper or a dull knife,
removing the hair and scurf before the final
butchering.

Each time I visit my brother in prison,
which sad to admit isn't as often as I would like
or as I should, I feel like I'm that little boy, wide-
eyed, sweaty, and shaking at the vat and then

hearing the shot—the slamming of prison doors—that starts the slaughter.

After the rest of the family relocated to Milwaukee I stayed behind with Hawk for two reasons. One was that we thought it was important that I finish school in East St. Louis because I was on track to go to college, and two, arthritis had begun to set in and Hawk couldn't do as much as he used to. I could still break a car down, load the truck, and go to school. On many occasions all he had left to do was drive. Although we tried to stay connected over time, our paths separated and we lost touch with one another.

I loved him and respected him. I felt like I owed him for the protection, for the advice, for the strength and lessons—from the slaughter. It's a difficult thing for my siblings to understand. My brother didn't get a chance to know his father. By the time they'd moved to Milwaukee, violence, deceit and abuse spread venom over the family. It was laid thick. And truth be told, it has left us all screaming on the inside like stuck hogs.

AND THE DOORS SLAM TO OPEN

Life's peppered with let-down, discouragement, and failure. It grows thick along the road like wild vines. But disappointment is only meant to slow your journey, not abate it, and it often precedes the elation of achievement and success. In fact, the chopping through, the swinging motion makes you stronger. Staying focused on what's on the other side gets you through the thickness of the brush and hydrates your bones.

Masks are good for hiding disappointment or protecting yourself from it. The poet Paul Laurence Dunbar penned a magnificent poem to this point. It reads:

We wear the mask that grins and lies,
It hides our cheeks and shades our eyes—
This debt we pay to human guile;
With torn and bleeding hearts we smile
And mouth with myriad subtleties.

Why should the world be over-wise,
In counting all our tears and sighs?
Nay, let them only see us while
We wear the mask.

We smile, but oh great Christ, our cries
To Thee from tortured souls arise.

We sing, but oh the clay is vile
Beneath our feet, and long the mile;
But let the world dream otherwise,
We wear the mask!ⁱⁱ

The contours and texture of your mask
will be crafted from your own family history,
personal hardships, and joys, and it will be shaped
by an intense desire to protect your dreams.
Looking at Dunbar's poem, it clearly seems that
he believed the mask to be worn by people of
color to hide their true selves from a wicked
world of White racism.

To a great extent, this will be true. Those
young men struggling to make a full recovery
from the legacy of slavery and purge its remnants
from the blood's memory will wear a mask that is
only meant for White folks to see. You will also
find that you will wear a mask that is only meant
for Blacks folks or non-Whites to see as well.

Being Black, I learned the hard way
growing up that there are two masks we must
carry. One mask you wear for a White world that
can very easily be ignorant of our history and
fearful of our capabilities. And one you wear for a
Black world that can lie in the same cesspool of
ignorance. White racism is easy to define, deal
with, and make some sense of, because it is
external to you. Black self-loathing, however, is
more difficult to handle. Anyone who has ever
been told they were "acting White" because of
their academic pursuits or "working in the White

man's world" because of their career choices
knows exactly what I am speaking of.

*How dare you want more, How dare you
fight harder, work smarter, talk different... How
dare you be different, live over there, talk to
them... How dare you dress like that, listen to
that music, and eat that food...How dare you
love that girl, embrace that faith...How dare you
break the cycle of an impoverished mind and
spirit and seek answers to questions we dare not
ask... How dare you?*

The ignorance of a crippled mind allows
people to think this way. It is also fear. Fear of
what other people may think or expect of them.
What we must grasp is that there is no "White
man's world." There is simply a world, and it is
filled with possibility; we can either cease our
greatest potential and promise or surrender. For
as much as your mask may protect you, it can also
suffocate.

If you're not careful, a poorly fitting or
overused mask can stifle, if not fully cut off, your
breathing. The air you take in through an ill-
fitted mask will taste stale and harsh to the
tongue. It can ruin all taste for living.

You'll have to learn when not to wear the
mask—when to leave it at home. In other words,
you'll have to learn when to be vulnerable and
open to life's bitterness and unexpected sweetness.
When to pocket the mask—keeping it close, just

Joseph F. West

in case, but with a willingness to let go and feel something new, no matter how frightening that may seem.

I first learned to wear my mask while at the University of Illinois. But it didn't fit well. It was loose around the edges and chafed my sensibilities. It's hard to study with a mask on. It can blur your understanding of the facts both inside books and outside, where folks come together and separate for all kinds of reasons. You try to fit into this group or that, each with its own identity and politics, and your mask becomes a symbol at times for some purpose completely unrelated to you that serves that of a group. It can lead you to draw senseless boundaries between friends and place limits on yourself. As young Black men we're all lumps of messy clay flopping around on a potter's lathe. Time, the right pace, a discerning eye, and a caring hand are all we need to help us pull it all together.

After I left the U of I, I worked with families as a social worker, appearing in courtrooms with child welfare lawyers, advocating at custody hearings, and laboring with guardians over what we thought was best for a child or children that maybe we'd see once a month.

The abuse and neglect was unimaginable, even for me. Soon I recognized that all social workers used their jobs to exercise some demons that held them captive, some pain or trauma they couldn't quite shake or couldn't quite accept. For some this yielded immense compassion and fair decision-making, while others acted out on vendettas against a system, a father, a mother, a grandparent, or a school, never actually seeing the child before them, only themselves. Social work can be a constant scraping and bandaging of a scar, never solving a problem—neither the client's nor our own. Like a patchwork quilt with meaningless patterns of worn-out patches that don't quite stitch well and stay frayed at the edges.

Out of sheer ambition or gross naivety, I kept at it, working to make a difference, and sometimes I actually did. Changing a situation or making someone's life better makes you soar inside for a brief moment, only to return to earth to face an entirely new set of challenges.

***

I wanted to be an academic. At the U of I, my interests shifted from agriculture to human culture. I liked the feel of a college campus, liked being around books, thinking people, and the energy of intellectual pursuit. Also the "Little Professor" title from childhood stuck. I kept working as a social worker and began taking classes in the evening at Roosevelt University in downtown Chicago to keep feeding my desire for learning. And here was where a lump of clay was handed to master craftsmen.

While at Roosevelt I met and became great friends with Dr. Kirk Harris. He was the first Black man I had ever met that had both a doctor of philosophy (Ph.D.) and a juris doctorate (J.D.). Dr. Harris kindled my desire to pursue a doctorate and helped me really get serious about the process.

I left social work and worked for Dr. Harris on some policy issues related to fatherhood and its impact on young people. My abilities were very raw and ill formed. But he stuck with me and emphasized certain skills in communication, thoroughness, and presence that would prove essential. While working for Dr. Harris, I learned of a study Harvard was conducting in Chicago. We discussed it and thought it would be a great opportunity for me to learn research from the ground up.

I applied, and after my first interview I met Dr. John Holton, another Black man in a leadership position. Dr. Holton was the executive director of the study, which followed young people over a period of eight to ten years to answer a question of how where a person grows up shapes who they are. Dr. Holton and I connected on two fronts, chess and jazz. He hired me right then, and shortly after that I was into the work. I became engrossed and as a fledgling researcher looked forward to going out into the Chicago streets each day listening to hundreds of people talk about where and how they lived.

Now, to me, both Kirk and John were
"cool." I mean a deep "cool" that melds intellect,
self-confidence, insight, and decisiveness that up
until that point I had not seen. With them there
was a Black male bravado with purpose that
thumped hard like an upright bass swung in
tempo.

Kirk later helped me reconnect with Dr.
Phillip Bowman, whom I'd known from the U of
I. Dr. Bowman, too, had the same "cool," but
Phil was more of a drummer. He favored a trap
set protagonist of protest and pragmatic
intellectualism. Phil played a powerful role in the
lives of dozens of young Black people completing
doctoral programs. He organized support groups
that routinely met to make sure we *finished* the
programs that so many of us had fought to be
accepted into.

I had a very strong trio in Kirk, John, and
Phil writing letters of recommendation, reading
personal statements, and helping me decide which
programs would be the best for my interests. We
came up with ten programs, yes, ten, and to their
credit they wrote letters for each one of them—
the measure of their commitment to me. In order
to strengthen my position, I took the Graduate
Record Exam four times, each time only raising
my score a few points. In the middle of this
flurry, John recommended that I speak to
someone else about my plans, someone who
would make a great fourth member, a quartet.

Dr. Felton Earls (Tony) is the ultimate jazzman, with roots to both New Orleans and Memphis, and a world-renowned and respected child psychiatrist and humanitarian. The study I was working on was his brainchild. I'd only met him, like everyone else who worked there, when he arrived from Boston for scientific meetings and to check in on things. He was very approachable, but there was no way I thought he would extend himself to me in this manner.

It took several pushes from John, but I spoke up, and much to my surprise Tony was excited to help. In fact, he spent time listening intently on several occasions as we discussed my background and research interests. Each time he came to town he'd make time to talk with me about staying on task and learning as much as I could about the work we were doing. I thought he would help review my personal statement or write a letter of recommendation; he threw me for a big loop when he suggested that I consider applying to the Harvard School of Public Health. I'd flunked out of U of I as a freshman, barely gotten back in, and fought my way to graduation. Harvard was not on my horizon.

Up until that point I had already received three rejection letters, including one from my alma mater, Illinois. My support band came together and said, "Why not, what would it hurt?" We decided to do it. I place emphasis on *we* because it was truly a group effort.

There was mounting uncertainty. I
received a fourth, fifth, and then a sixth rejection
letter. The Harvard application was the eleventh
application submitted. Soon I had received eight
rejection letters, and of the three remaining
applications, two were top-tier programs,
including Harvard. I felt I had a snowball's
chance in hell of getting in there, and the other
two were so far from Chicago I had grown
increasingly uncertain of whether I would go even
if accepted. When the doors slam, it's more than
just your face in it, it's your sense of self-worth,
your dreams, and desires being rejected, pushed
aside. It's a dirgeful suffering.

The rejection letters piled up, and
needling thoughts of "scholarly deficiency"
started to creep in. I talked with the quartet and
shared how I was feeling. They never let me stay
down. Had it not been for their continued
support and encouragement, I could have easily
revisited some very dark places.

To relax, I was playing jazz trumpet at
the time. I hung out in jazz clubs across Chicago
and the Midwest. I was exhausted mentally and
physically and could only muster enough strength
to spend some ungodly hours playing blues and
swing—jam session after jam session. Perhaps as
an illusionary joke to myself, I thought of packing
my horn and roaming the country from the bayou
to the back hills sleeping, walking, and talking the
blues had I not gotten into a graduate program.
Two high marks for me were playing in jam

sessions with the elegant trumpeter Wynton Marsalis, whom I modeled much of my playing after by transcribing and practicing his solos, and talented guitarist Mark Whitfield. As any devoted musician will confess: the blues, she's a strange mistress. She won't stand for you loving anything, and at times anyone else, but her. My commitment didn't run that deep, so I let the fleeting thought roll by.

I felt like I was stumbling around in a thick, scratchy fog of discord and dissonance. In total, ten schools rejected me. Late winter or early spring (you never know which is which in Chicago) I received an acceptance letter from Harvard, the only one I would receive. The fog cleared. After leaving the University of Illinois, I learned to manage my mask pretty well, allowing myself to grow into myself—which was a constant process of slow, deliberate steps and missteps. The graduate school application process allowed me to travel quite a distance within myself, being open to the possibilities, accepting constant growth and the failures that came with the trip. Entering Harvard I struggled with my mask again, though, because it required a more customized fit.

I knew I had a very strong trio. But when it became a quartet, I felt it was beyond us. There was another force at work—God. It had to be. That was the only way I could wrap my head around the idea that four Black men of that caliber would commit themselves to me, a twenty-something with no proven ability but in their eyes some promise. I don't think it was lost on anyone the weight Dr. Earls' influence brought to the band. I am eternally grateful for each of them. Growing up along the Mississippi, I once heard an old man say that the only thing a Black man can do by himself is fail. I wasn't alone, and I was determined not to fail.

The appreciation of music helps you respect time—its freedom and order. There's only so much room to pace, caress and bend notes to your will and tastes. And when you've found your cadence, settled into your groove, there's peace in knowing that you can't fall out of time.

ON THE CHARLES

I entered Harvard in September of 1999. I'd arrived in Massachusetts about 4:00 a.m. driving fifteen hours straight from Chicago. The drive on Interstate 90 East is phenomenal. The flat prairie of the Midwest gives way to the Eastern Hills of Pennsylvania, New York, and Massachusetts. It's best to map the drive during the early fall, when the sky explodes with color from the foliage.

I was newly married at the time, and my wife and I rode through the empty streets of Cambridge, stumbling upon Harvard Square. It was a good thing that it was so early in the morning because my internal compass had to adjust to the narrow, one-way streets and loops. We parked the car on Massachusetts Avenue in front of the Harvard bookstore and began to walk around Harvard Yard. We entered Johnston Gate, and immediately I was taken by the architecture. Bubbling with excitement and a deep sense of relief, I rubbed John Harvard Statue. Then we stood inside Memorial Church where I offered a quick prayer of thanks.

Finally I ran up the stairs of Widener Library steps and jumped around like Rocky

Balboa. Perhaps it was the damp cool of a
September morning mixed with the flush warm
pride of achievement, but Harvard felt right. I
took it all in. Harvard Yard was a far cry from
dusty playgrounds and sewage of East St. Louis
and the noise and vagrancy of Chicago's
Westside. I knew there was a lot still to
accomplish, and arriving safely after driving all
day and into the night was but a tiny step
forward. However, unlike during my
undergraduate years, I wasn't afraid.

We were all set to move into an
apartment along Mt. Auburn Street, which runs
parallel to the Charles River. Shaler Lane is a
picturesque, tree-lined cove of a street made up of
family townhomes and apartments. We didn't
have our keys yet, and the U-Haul was still
attached to the back of the Volkswagen, so we
parked on a back street and strolled down our
new block. We were awash with happiness and
nervous about what the future held. I could tell
my wife was pleased with the surroundings.

Prior to arriving at Harvard, I'd seen
many pictures of the Charles River and knew that
it ran between Cambridge and Boston and
alongside MIT. Here it was now, right across the
street from our new home. We only needed to
cross a small park and Memorial Drive, and we
were right there. We'd later learned that on
Sundays Memorial Drive would close and people
would run, stroll, skate, row, and ride up and
down the drive. We walked around our new

neighborhood and crossed through the park to take a peep downriver. We had a few more hours to burn, so we continued to become familiar with the place where a new set of joys, friends, successes, and failures awaited.

A co-worker from Chicago had moved to Boston to study and work the previous year. We met her for breakfast at a small diner. We met in Porter Square, and while having breakfast I heard at least three different dialects and a few people speaking English with rich accents. Outside of the aesthetic feel of Cambridge, I appreciated the city's intense diversity. For the first time I was truly in a global community, a far cry from the segregation of southern Illinois and Chicago.

Against the undertone of clanging silverware and the quiet rumble of a crowded morning time slot, the peppered conversations helped set a great tone for the day—and for my entire time in Massachusetts. I came to appreciate the many different foods, clothing, libations, and cultural practices of people from the world over. Without question this added to my learning. Experiencing the richness of life as told through the words and deeds of others gave me a profound appreciation of global citizenship.

Finishing breakfast, we picked up our keys to the apartment and quickly unloaded the small U-Haul stuffed to the seams with our humble belongings. After we made short order of the packing, my wife was exhausted and pleaded

for a nap. Restless, I continued to unpack then
returned the U-Haul. I had spent the better part
of my now-ten hours on one side of the Charles
River; I anxiously wanted to cross over into
Boston.

The Harvard School of Public Health
sits nestled in what's called the Longwood
Medical Area, a quadrangle of medicine and
science alongside Harvard Medical and Dental
Schools. The imposing neoclassical marble
stretches along Longwood Avenue and connects
to Beth Israel Deaconess Medical Center, Brigham
and Women's Hospital, Dana Farber Cancer
Institute, and Children's Hospital. It's an
environment ripe for the pursuit of knowledge. I
soon learned it was also a place ripe for
insecurities, ignorance, and the promulgation of
inadequacy—*the muck,* I'd come to call it, to
own it, to foster it, to bury myself in it, to loathe
it—and come to overcome it.

I walked down Huntington Avenue
toward the School of Public Health. The first
building I saw was the François-Xavier Bagnoud
(FXB) Center for Health and the Human Rights
building. Inscribed on the outside of the building
is a statement that everyone has a fundamental
right to the highest standard of public health.
When I first saw it, I thought it was an
impressive, if not lofty, edict. After years of study
I developed a profound appreciation for its
meaning and how difficult the fundamental right

to be healthy and have an equal opportunity to thrive really is—in America and elsewhere.

I'd been awake nearly twenty hours at this point. After walking around Longwood Medical Area for a half hour or so, I went back across the river to Cambridge to make one more visit before going home to get some sleep. I had to go by Harvard Law School.

Once I got my acceptance letter to Harvard, a friend of mine sent me a copy of *Why Should White Guys Have All the Fun?* It is a powerful story about Reginald Lewis, one of the country's first African-American business powerhouses who amassed a fortune of four hundred million and led the billion-dollar buyout of Beatrice International. He was an incredibly driven, smart, and creative person, evidenced by his being the first student accepted to Harvard's Law School without submitting an application. Before passing away from brain cancer, he'd become a philanthropist, giving several million dollars to Harvard Law, which established the Reginald F. Lewis International Law Center, the first major facility at Harvard named in honor of an African-American.

I was anxious to see his portrait hanging inside the center. Looking at Reginald Lewis' portrait, I began to imagine his deep sense to achieve, his desire to dominate, and his obligation to be a symbol. I had no notions of being a multimillionaire like Lewis. I was entering into public health, where the financial rewards are modest at best. Yet I admired his dogged determinism.

***

My first day at the Harvard School of Public Health was a stifling blend of excitement and stark reality. I was anxious to schedule my classes. I had initially applied to the doctoral program, but was accepted as a master's student first. I was taken aback by how few men there were in my program, and how few African-American men there were on campus, period. I also later discovered how few African-American men had completed the master's program and that there had not been any to complete the doctoral program prior to me.

After completing my class schedule, there was the daunting task of how I was going to pay for school. I took out loans and more loans each year, telling myself it was an investment in me and that I would repay myself many times over. Eventually I received a couple of scholarships, namely the Dwight D. Eisenhower scholarship, which helped with reducing the amount of loans I took, even going one year not needing a loan at all. There were wonderful staff in academic affairs and financial services that made it a point to help students find money, apply for scholarships, and work out the best loan options. This relieved much of the anxiety.

After working out a plan for how I would pay for my first year, I went to purchase my books. Sitting down in a coffee shop with my Harvard COOP bags filled with books and supplies, I felt like a twelve-year-old just starting junior high—getting my locker for the first time, scheduling my own classes for the first time. Although I'd completed college, it was as if I'd just finished sixth grade and was deemed a gifted child all over again. Flipping through the textbooks, I realized how much I didn't know and how hard I would have to work.

Classes began, and at first I felt a little like I felt the first days at U of I—a little out of place. It was one thing to complete my coursework, and something entirely different to be working on a career course. It was the first time I came to know the real difference between having a job, which most people do, and having a body of work, by which you're ultimately measured. Colleagues and instructors were always asking, "What are you working on?" It took a while to get accustomed to the idea of always having something to "work on." I thought having to study was enough, but it isn't. When swimming in a pond of chronic overachievers, as in a school of goldfish, you needed to always be swimming furiously toward something. I never really thought of myself as such a fish, the pressure mounted for me to define my work early. "Where will your contribution be?" was the question being pounded at me, and "Will it be worth acknowledging?" was the force behind it. If

I felt very insecure, alone, or facing other pressing personal issues, the question could dreadfully morph into "Am I worth acknowledging?"

A number of suicides have occurred at Harvard. There were at least two I can recall on the Medical Area Campus during my time. I'd already been down that road and had no desire to revisit it, but many more students became depressed and despondent. These students tended to leave their programs, either on their own or after being asked to leave. Students that didn't have the support of family, friends, or instructors would flap in the wind a while, break off, and disappear over the horizon. You never knew who was having trouble until one day they were gone, either returning home, embarking on a new career choice, or simply decided to wander and "find themselves" all over again.

I'd been doing some of the groundwork in Chicago with Kirk, John, Phil, and Tony. The problem for me was twofold. One was knowing when and where to start, as I was rather comfortable on the "how," given my previous community work. The other problem was more daunting: knowing whether or not it would be considered "serious" or valid work.

Improving the health of African-American men was where I wanted my contribution to be. I wasn't really sure what that meant; I only knew this was the area in which I wanted to focus my work. So I began talking to anyone who'd listen and thinking through how I would approach the number of issues out there. I took a brave step forward and organized a forum on the health of African-American men. I didn't have an organization or much to work with, but I identified some key people in the community and on Harvard's campus, reserved a lecture hall, put together a brief program, and sent out letters inviting anyone interested in listening and talking about the issues to come.

I hadn't been in Boston long at all and didn't have any connections in the community. I had no idea what I was doing, but I just knew I had to do it. It wrenched in my gut for weeks and it turned out to be one of the best things I'd ever done while there. The day the event was to occur, the lecture hall was at first rather empty; then it slowly filled up with educators, instructors, a dean, a public health commissioner, social workers, physicians, researchers, and everyday folk.

Most were interested in the topic, while others wanted to know who this guy was with no credentials and who had invited the community to campus. Little did I know the Longwood Medical Area had a reputation of seeming "off-limits" to adjacent communities like Roxbury, for example. Architecturally, there are no entrances that face the outside community, so from that vantage point it can seem physically closed. The conversation about the lives and well-being of Black men needed to be opened—and needed to

be opened there at the Harvard School of Public
Health. At the forum, the dialogue and exchange
was exciting and confirmed for me that the issue
was indeed relevant. It also taught me that I was
considered as serious or valid as my dedication
and effort.

The public health commissioner of
Cambridge, Harold Cox, was in attendance.
Harold has an energetic and bright, smiling face
with purposeful eyes. Following the forum he
offered me an opportunity to meet with him and
discuss his Men of Color Health Initiative. The
initiative had existed for a couple of years in many
different forms. I came on board first to learn,
and then to assist.

Harold had invited me to be a part of
what could only be described as a family. The
office in Cambridge was a pleasant blend of
surrogate mothers and sisters who watched out
and watched over me. I struggled to mold
together my early community organizing
experience, what I was learning from the people,
with what I was learning in the classroom. This
was the start of me finding my self-confidence—
and finding another mentor. Under Harold's
guidance and insight, I grew my understanding of
what a practicing public health leader really was. I
always say he taught me to argue for what's right
graciously.

I had two other mentors: Tony, who
continued to stay with me chairing my doctoral

committee and supervising my research efforts, and Augustus A. White, who talked with me a lot about my obligation to succeed and seeking excellence in my work. They both also emphasized that I work on my own timetable, work hard, but don't allow other's pace to set mine. I was a mutt-mix of raw ore material forged by craftsmen of science and virtue. In concert they tenaciously hammered at me to be a better collector of knowledge and formulator of ideas. Each was interested in my success as a man. They were brutally honest with me when I slacked off, produced subpar results, or became too unfocused, and measured their praise when I made a strong stride forward. It was an experience wrought with its own challenges and disappointments. Like a splash of cool water to hot metal, the sizzle and steam of life's unsettling moments rose on occasion. The shock and rush of the sudden rise of change caused me at times to deform, spill over the mold, and bend.

One such moment occurred while I was struggling to begin my doctoral program. I found myself in a painful situation where my marriage was crumbling. During this same time, I received a call that my youngest brother had been arrested for homicide. Both required my immediate attention. I was unsuccessful at saving either.

It was late one May, and the newness of a New England spring still lingered as I left Logan Airport bound for Chicago, where my best friend, Ernest, picked me up. He insisted on going with

me to Milwaukee to see my sixteen-year-old
brother for the first time behind glass in the
visitation room of the jail. Ernest Kamara, a
native of Sierra Leone who is from a big family
with many obligations, was then and is today my
brother in every sense. We lived in the same
residence hall as undergraduates and vowed to
help each other realize our dreams. He was in his
medical residency at the time and had himself
overcome many obstacles. As we drove from
O'Hare to Milwaukee, he listened as I rambled to
try to make sense of what I was about to see and
what I was going through.

Witnessed tragedy reveals the brisk
connection between eyes and heart. A familiar
child wearing a burnt orange jumpsuit sat down
in front of me behind thick-wired glass, pick up a
stainless steel phone, and spoke. My heart
shattered and my eyes labored to detain the flood.
We talked about this and that, skirting emotion,
running from the impending. He began to
murmur to me the confluence of events that led
us to where we could only look at one another's
ears to listen and avoid the deluge of tears.

His father visited him that day, the last
time they would see each other. I made several
trips to visit and attend his sentencing, but I went
back to Boston to work on school and home. I
couldn't afford to travel back and forth that often
and missed most of the trial. Life plus forty-two
years was his sentence to Wisconsin Correctional
System. You don't know quite how to take the

crushing dislodge to your own senses when you hear it. It sounds fictional, the "plus forty-two years." You don't expect to have more years than what God has promised, and you don't know what he has promised you. The state wanted that and then some. Though my brother would be alive, the sound of the final gavel shook the living from me. Here I was in Boston working on the well-being of Black men and I couldn't help my own brother.

Home was fizzling and school was so peripheral. I felt I was only doing a little better than my brother, but truth knows better than to compare. Worse yet, I was preparing for my written qualifying exams, which would determine whether I would press on with my doctoral work or be sent packing.

It's impossible to study methodology, theory, and practice when your head is filled with the echoing guilt of "Had I...had I...had I..." Had I worked more on being a better husband, listening more, paying my wife more attention—had I spent more time with my brother—I could have avoided simultaneous collapse.

I took a battered heart and an unfocused mind into my written exams. Through the first part of the exam, I kept thinking that my being there was the cause of why things had fallen apart. I wrote my name and scribbled at some questions. I was an unconscious mess. At intermission I sat foggy in the courtyard, and before I knew it, the

time to return had passed. I didn't return to take
the rest of my exam. Instead I wandered back
across the river on foot, convinced I was finished
with school.

MAKING THE TURN UP

I came to appreciate Harvard, the myth and the reality. Sculling along the Charles, famous professors, late summer getaways to Martha's Vineyard, the rich diversity of the people, the antiquated beauty of Cambridge, the decadence of the grounds, the thinly veiled air of elitism, and even the financial sacrifice and academic failure were all valued. The Charles was no Mississippi, though. For as formidable as the waves and wash were, I'd overcome worse undertows, so I shook off the silt and marched back to the School of Public Health.

I was surprised at the support I received. Several of the professors in the department expressed how much they'd believed in me from the start and were pleased that I'd decided to continue. Some even shared stories of their own graduate school trials. They wanted to help me succeed and respected that even though I'd fallen flat on my face, more than once, I was willing to get up, bloody nose and all, and press on. It was no sprint, for sure. I was to wait a year and retake the written exam, while my cohort was to move on. I didn't mind this. It allowed me a chance to continue to get my personal life in order and to focus on studying.

Things were going very well for me during the final two years of my doctoral program. The high point was I was able to be a teaching fellow for the preeminent scholar Cornel West. Like me he has roots in Oklahoma and we often discussed common threads that ran between us in this regard. It was difficult for students to understand where he was coming from, and it was our job as teaching fellows to help them better understand, as well as guide them through the intense reading list and grade assignments. Students were intoxicated, enthralled, and enlightened by his powerful and poetic prose that lifted their spirits and challenged them in ways they'd never imagined.

West was then and still is today a lightening rod. He's drawn fire for some of his comments such as those following the attacks of September 11, 2001. Not long after that he battled with then–Harvard president Lawrence Summers and subsequently left Harvard to return to Princeton. West and I had lunch the week of his exchange with Summers and what I saw in his face and heard in his words was what I'd also taken in from my aforementioned quartet and other mentors—there's an impermanent cloak of respect for Black men that, when snatched back, burns and bruises.

We discussed the metaphysical and visceral nature of the blues as idiomatic of the complicated yet robust feelings Black men have regarding their own success.

There's duplicity in the blues that on the one hand speaks of progression while at the same time hollering out loud to take small half-steps back to reflect on the meaning of grounds vacated and the purpose of the space being filled. It's perhaps something only musicians, scientists, philosophers, preachers, or the formerly incarcerated can appreciate. Or, to quote the artist Lauryn Hill from the song "Superstar," "First they hail you then they nail you."

This was a watershed moment for me, and as graduation approached my reflections on West, Tony, Kirk, Phil, Gus, John, and others reminded me of something John Henrik Clarke, the noted Pan-Africanist American writer, historian, and professor, once said to me as an undergraduate. In the early nineties I had the pleasure of serving as one of the hosts for Dr. Clarke during a visit to the U of I. We were preparing for dinner and I shared with him my budding interest to pursue a doctorate degree. He said, "Young man, never forget that the man that gave out the first PhD never had one. Knowledge is organic once you're able to connect to your actual self, and wisdom is acquired over a long, long, time of self-study."

Graduation was a bittersweet experience. The bitter was that my graduate advisor Lawren Daltroy had died a few months before from a recurrence of melanoma. As his last student, I spoke at his memorial the day before I was to take my oral exam, which is the final exam in the doctoral program. I dedicated the exam presentation to him and got through it successfully. Deborah Prothrow-Stith, the former Commissioner of Public Health for Massachusetts and Assistant Dean; Steve Gortmaker, department professor; and Tony made up my doctoral committee. Oral exams are open to the public so my uncle Mike, some friends, and other guests were in attendance. A few moments after my exam we celebrated in the department with some champagne and food.

Graduation day was festive and full of pageantry, as every Harvard graduation seems to be. The day started in Cambridge in Harvard Yard for the university commencement, and later culminated in Boston for the School of Public Health degree conferment. The School of Public Health has a commencement tradition of awarding each graduate a copy of the Universal Declaration of Human Rights, which when my name was called was handed to my daughter. The picture made the papers.

I've worked hard to continue to serve humanity through my work as an epidemiologist, businessman, and author, and through my fraternity Phi Beta Sigma. While in Boston I was awarded the Albert Schweitzer "Reverence for Life" Award. The award is given to the student that demonstrates a commitment to service and "making their life an argument" in much the same way as the namesake humanitarian and Nobel laureate.

I've since returned to North Lawndale where I am working to improve the health of the community by eliminating racist tobacco ads, getting people to try to eat healthier, exercise more, better manage current illness and eliminate community violence. This has also meant working for better public health clinics and community outreach as well as fighting for the universal right to quality health care.

Part of the lesson of spending some time on a farm is that you learn that if you plan poorly, you will yield poorly. There will be seasons where nature scraps your plans, laughs at your efforts, and tests your resolve by producing no yield. The main lesson is that everyone who enjoys the comforts and bounty of the harvest must be a part of executing the plan—contribute in some meaningful way to the preparation, planting, and picking. There were times when the elders in my family would emphasize that if you didn't work or help out, you didn't eat. This isn't to say that family or guests or strangers, no matter their contribution, wouldn't be able to sit at the table and enjoy a great meal and feel welcome. It did mean, though, if some people in the house had to be up at 5:00 a.m. working, everyone had to be up at 5:00 a.m. doing something that would benefit the whole.

As children we were not allowed to walk down the street and walk past litter on the sidewalk or in the street. Some elder would kindly ask that you deposed of the trash. Although in most instances you were not responsible for dropping the litter, you did have a responsibility to keep where you lived clean because that was where you lived, and what was on the street was a representation of you and a reflection of what you were learning in your home. The idea here is that at times we wrestle with this notion of who we are to ourselves and to each other.

Another rewarding aspect of my work has been the great fortune of being able to speak to men ages six to sixty—men from all hues and areas of life. This audience has allowed me to speak to them about my trials and triumphs, and in equal exchange listen to their stories. In many special instances I've been invited to venture deep into their hearts and hear songs of tribulation and victory. There have been times where I've heard the continuation of a question asked by ten-year-old with the answer still being sought by someone several decades older. Intimately timeless queries of this magnitude are quite often ones pertaining to our humanity, connection and disconnection to others, purpose and destiny, and most of all love—that most tender, healing, duplicitous, ethereal, and longed-for blue note of them all.

I am not sure if this is folklore, but I was once told that as Harriet Tubman lead slaves on the Underground Railroad, she carried a Bible in one hand and a pistol in the other. Traveling the Underground Railroad was a difficult journey where hunger, swamps, hiding, and the ever-present fear of what would happen should you be caught would shake anyone's faith, in God and themselves. It's imaginable that her Bible was needed to offer comfort to the faithful, and the pistol served to encourage those who lost faith to keep moving because she was determined not to leave anybody behind. Upon reaching freedom and feeling release from proverbial and unseen shackles, the faithful rejoiced and praised the Lord. Those who lost faith along the way also rejoiced and were grateful for the little push forward toward a better place Ms. Tubman knew existed, but they couldn't see. And this is a bit how I see myself and my argument in life. That's to say, as an imperfect creature, to walk with a lasting faith in God and to be unyielding in my resolve to keep moving.

I've climbed upward and onward, literally and figuratively, taking in the journey along the way, knowing that it's incomplete. My taste for adventure and the outdoors has opened my eyes to my own physical and spiritual limitations. I often say to people if you want to know just how insignificant you are, spend some time outside in the wilderness. Nature quickly humbles. A couple of years ago I climbed Mount Rainier, a glacier covered mountain just outside of Seattle, Washington that stands at 14, 411 feet. When I arrived in Seattle I was bursting with excitement as I made my way to the Whitaker Rainier

Mountaineering BaseCamp where I had a chance to meet Lou Whitaker. A tall man with hands like carved granite, Lou led the first successful summit of the North Col of Mount Everest. He's climbed Mount Rainier about 250 times and in his mid seventies he appeared to be the fittest man there. I've known professional athletes, football and baseball players mostly—so I've seen strong. But mountaineers, ranchers and fishermen possess an incomparable strength. A might forged by the rigors of Mother Nature.

Our group endured a blinding snow storm mid-way on our ascent to Camp Muir, the 10,000 foot stopover to the summit. Carrying fifty pound backpacks and each climber being able to see but a few feet ahead, we nearly jogged up the mountain to shelter where throughout the night winds crashed and howled while ice crackled and fell. Just prior to this mad dash up we'd taken a brief break in a clearing where in the distance the majesty and wonder of Mount St. Helens and Mount Adams captured every climber. Out of sheer awe and breathless admiration I penned the following:

Here I stand, ages from where I've been—
Smalled, humbled, in a plaid band
Taking it all in;
One step closer to me, to you and the ceiling above;
One step closer to God's love;

Cloudless the air—
Not like before,
Moorish dreams, here
Stepping through time's door;
A stride at my pace, hear
That only I can make;
Carving a lucid path, for renewal sake
One step closer to me, to you and the ceiling above;
One step closer to God's love.

I know now why prophets, poets and philosophers are summoned into the mountains. It's the elevation, the quiet exertion—the putting behind and letting go.

In climbing there's constant preparation for slipping, measuring your breath and discerning the best route forward. Each step is deliberate. It's a complete test of your endurance and commitment to that very moment. You have to find the long lines of yourself, the stretch inside. You make your way, learning to brace against the wind, and being prepared to make the next turn up.

A CODA BLUE

The air of lost hope has teeth, and when it blows it shreds. You must pay attention to all that surrounds you on the road. There will be detours, roadblocks, back streets, and hidden trails along the way. There will be charlatans, harlots, fortunetellers, wizards, trolls, and walking serpents.

Many of them will look like you. In fact, a number will come from your own family or community. They will claim to share the same values as you do and to have your best interest at heart—and some will. Many, however, won't. It's important that you be able to tell the difference; otherwise you may end up wandering waywardly into an abyss or a maze with no way out. Have a vision and make it plain. Own it and use it to plot your course.

Believe me, I am under no illusion. Half of you for whom these notes are offered may never see them or fully understand their purpose. Some of this will be due to a lack of effort on your part, and some to a lack of effort on the part of others. Some, not fully grasping what I'm saying, may have not only left the physical school building but also the school of life. Others are merely disengaged from abstract notions of America, responsibility, and manhood. And for

113

the remaining, nothing has ever really been abstract for you. On the other hand, it hasn't been concrete either.

It's quite easy to blame this disorientation on a political, social, and economic system replete with historical racial and geographic prejudice, and inequality. But to only find blame in a land marked by dragons and warlords would be to weaken your relevance over your own life. There will always be unfairness— some barrier or roadblock, a seemingly immovable stone.

Seek out the historical reference to and relevance of yourself—the hinge between what holds you up and what propels you forward. Without this as a map, there's an ever-increasing danger of tying and stepping into your own noose.

Lurking and omnipresent media place weakness and complacence on display, making it acceptable, marketable, even profitable behavior to minstrel and coon. "Crunk and drunk" is a castrating attempt at acceptance. To travel this way, the windows will shatter and the walls close in as you become an inept representation of the forefathers that made it possible for you to hold your head high.

It's about choices, making the best choices even from a poor set of choices. Because believe it or not, as you make better choices, the options before you become better. At birth there's no prison number stamped on your diaper or swaddling blanket. There may be a number inked on a shelf in some remote, mysterious, urban, or rural enclave. However, it is up to you to punch that bus ticket. Odds are you know where that bus is headed. You've either waved at a brother, cousin, uncle, or even a father as they boarded for their unfortunate trip, or you've visited them upon their dreadful arrival. So you're no stranger to how rough that road can be.

The challenge for each man on his own stony road is to learn to live with and through his choices. It will be here, young man, where the road will wind and dive, that you get stuck and want to turn around. And it's here that you will march on, shaking the earth like a herd of wondrous elephants. Don't choke on dry bones kicked up along the way or hide in the dust. Anger is the promulgation of elevated self-importance, and it leads to nothing but pain and suffering. Because what ails us sticks to the bones, learn to cope with your internal combustions of anger, angst, anxiety, and self-loathing. It's a choice to stand up or simply roll over and become roadkill.

Trod, young man, in the faith of your potential—it's your time. Shine and press on in the lucid warmth of promise, and dream big dreams, wish upon that star, and stroll in the glorious rhythm that only you possess.

Endnotes

---

[i] Authorship for the prayer has been attributed to Reinhold Niebuhr. See Sifton, Elizabeth (2005). *The Serenity Prayer: Faith and Politics in Times of Peace and War.* W. W. Norton & Company; Reprint edition (January 30, 2005).

[ii] "We Wear the Mask" is reprinted from *The Complete Poems of Paul Laurence Dunbar.* Paul Laurence Dunbar. New York: Dodd, Mead, and Co., 1913.

Made in the USA
Lexington, KY
12 February 2013